CHARLIE FALKNER is an Australian playwright from Sydney, New South Wales. His first full-length play, *Dirty People* premiered in Sydney and was subsequently staged across Australia, including seasons in Melbourne, Perth, and Adelaide. It was published in 2017. His second play, *Sex Object*, secured an off-Broadway run in New York City in 2018 and was published in 2019 by Australian Plays Transform. Falkner's plays have been showcased at the Sydney Fringe Comedy Festival, Perth FringeWorld, Belvoir St Theatre, The Pit (NYC) and The IRT (NYC) among others. As the co-Artistic director of JackRabbit Productions, Charlie has produced over sixteen new works across Australia. He is a graduate of the University of Sydney and the Australian Film, Television and Radio School.

CURRENCY PLAYS

First published in 2024
by Currency Press Pty Ltd,
Gadigal Land, Suite 310, 46–56 Kippax Street, Surry Hills, NSW 2010, Australia
enquiries@currency.com.au
www.currency.com.au

Copyright: *Introduction* © Hilary Bell, 2024; *Darwin's Reptilia* © Charlie Falkner, 2024.

COPYING FOR EDUCATIONAL PURPOSES

The Australian *Copyright Act 1968* [Act] allows a maximum of one chapter or 10% of this book, whichever is the greater, to be copied by any educational institution for its educational purposes provided that that educational institution [or the body that administers it] has given a remuneration notice to Copyright Agency [CA] under the Act.

For details of the CA licence for educational institutions contact CA, 12/66 Goulburn Street, Sydney, NSW, 2000; tel: within Australia 1800 066 844 toll free; outside Australia 61 2 9394 7600; fax: 61 2 9394 7601; email: memberservices@copyright.com.au

COPYING FOR OTHER PURPOSES

Except as permitted under the Act, for example a fair dealing for the purposes of study, research, criticism or review, no part of this book may be reproduced, stored in a retrieval system, or transmitted in any form or by any means without prior written permission. All enquiries should be made to the publisher at the address above.
Any performance or public reading of *Darwin's Reptilia* is forbidden unless a licence has been received from the author or the author's agent. The purchase of this book in no way gives the purchaser the right to perform the play in public, whether by means of a staged production or a reading. All applications for public performance should be addressed to the author c/–Currency Press

Typeset by Brighton Gray for Currency Press.
Cover design by Col McElwaine for Currency Press.

Currency Press acknowledges the Traditional Owners of the Country on which we live and work. We pay our respects to all Aboriginal and Torres Strait Islander Elders, past and present.

A catalogue record for this book is available from the National Library of Australia

Contents

Introduction vii
  Hilary Bell

DARWIN'S REPTILIA 1

Danny Ball, Ainslie McGlynn and Mathew Lee in Belvoir 25A's Darwin's Reptilia, *2023 (Photo: Philip Erbarcher)*

Zoe Jensen and Leilani Loau in Belvoir 25A's Darwin's Reptilia, *2023 (Photo: Philip Erbarcher)*

Acknowledgment

I acknowledge the Traditional Owners of the land where I live and work. This play is set in Larrakia Country (Darwin), Australia, and I acknowledge the Larrakia people as the Traditional Owners of the region. I pay my respects to Larrakia elders past and present. I celebrate the stories, culture, and traditions of Aboriginal and Torres Strait Islander Elders of all communities who also work and live on this land.

I extend my celebration of the stories, culture, and traditions to Aboriginal and Torres Strait Islander Elders of all communities and lands across Australia.

Charlie Falkner

Ainslie McGlynn in Belvoir 25A's Darwin's Reptilia, *2023 (Photo: Philip Erbarcher)*

Introduction

The end of the world is nigh. In Darwin, the mangroves have been destroyed by an out-of-control climate, and with nowhere else to go, the crocodiles—usually a tourist attraction at Crocosaurus Cove—have gone rogue and are infiltrating the city. The inhabitants have been ordered to lock their gates and hole up inside. Trapped in the 'withered' Palms Motel are an assortment of desperate characters, vividly brought to life through Charlie Falkner's poetic, playful and very funny dialogue. These are manager Bobbi, employee Flick (who never seems to do any work), guests Renata and Declan, from New York and Galway respectively, and John from Pennsylvania. There's also Declan and Renata's addendum of a baby, who, as the outcome of a one-night-stand, beautifully embodies the play's themes of recklessness and accountability.

Early on in the play, Renata defends what her publisher predicts to be the Next Big Thing: 'selfique culture'. 'Just, you know—individualism or ... whatever. He likes capitalism. Freedom.' Falkner arranges his characters along the selfique spectrum, and through their relationships, examines the tension between taking responsibility and living with abandon at any cost. On a macro level, he is asking how the planet has reached this perilous point if not from a 'damn the consequences' attitude. These five characters, who, like the premise, are larger-than-life (but only slightly), wrestle with what it means to live to the fullest while dealing with the repercussions of their actions—or not, as the case may be. The world is in trouble, but does that mean we should let go of the reins and let it plunge into the abyss?

Renata, a self-help author who can't be accused of not practising what she preaches, is at the far end of the scale. Her book, *Life Off Leash: A Guide to Embracing Chaos*, encourages readers to liberate themselves and take a leap of faith into the unknown. To be free, she exhorts them, one must avoid parenthood. So it's ironic when she discovers she's five months pregnant. As a result of a wild affair initiated during a running with the bulls, she's stuck with a baby she doesn't want, and a humourless Irishman intent on turning her into a housewife. And certainly, Declan's insistence on trapping Renata into a life that clearly horrifies her is not going make any of them happy. Their relationship is encapsulated in the play's opening lines, as they fail miserably to communicate:

> DECLAN: Smoke.
> RENATA: What?
> DECLAN: Hm?
> RENATA: Smoke.
> DECLAN: You see that / smoke?
> RENATA: He's smoking.
> DECLAN: Yer. He's inside, so, just—how do you know him again?
> RENATA: That's Micah. I know Micah.
> DECLAN: Yes. How do you know him?
> RENATA: Micah?
> DECLAN: ... *Yes.*
> RENATA: He published it. He's in publishing. And a writer. He writes about / things.
> DECLAN: Don't like him. Obnoxious. Reminds me of—
> RENATA: Of what?
> DECLAN: Of smoking.
> RENATA: You smoke though.
> DECLAN: Ah? No. No I don't. What?
> RENATA: What?
> DECLAN: I don't do that. I tamed that beast.
> RENATA: Okay.
> DECLAN: Ah?
> RENATA: I said okay. You don't smoke. I thought you did.
> DECLAN: I quit, Ren. You didn't notice. Three weeks ago.

Darwin, as Flick tells us, is a place where drifters and runaways end up, as her mother did after giving birth to her own unwanted child, Flick's half-sister Renata, in America: 'Just left her so she didn't have to deal with it.'

Renata is simply following in her mother's footsteps. She doesn't seem to hold any grudge about being abandoned, though it's telling that in her world travels, she never came to Australia for a visit. When

Flick questions this, the most Renata will say is, 'Well she left me. I was a child. Wasn't going to come crawling back.'

This off-stage character, the mother of Renata and Flick, is the epitome of irresponsibility, and in her actions we see a reflection of the play's larger concerns. Flick explains to Renata what she was like: 'Mum used to say that. Let it burn! Like if she thought there was an easy way out. Mum used to camp a lot, like whenever she was kind of running away ... she was always on the move. And she would camp and set up these tents and then she'd get bored and want to come here or whatever so she'd just like burn the whole thing? Like burn the tent and everything inside and just come back? Like it never happened. Just leave all her burnt shit in the bush.' Renata's response is to laugh, and say, 'I like that. Let it burn.'

It's one thing to behave heedlessly if it has no effect on anybody else; however, Renata has legions of fans lapping up her advice, the thirstiest of all being John. Following the book's commands, he throws in his job and leaves his dying father in search of the bigger life he thinks he should be living. The results are both exhilarating and awful, and when he turns to Renata for answers, she washes her hands of him. Not her problem.

In terms of risk-taking, Flick is her sister's polar opposite. She has never set foot outside Darwin, sticking around to look after their errant mother. In a rare moment of vulnerability, Flick confides, 'She had me here when she didn't really know who she was. So, she couldn't really be my mum until she sorted that out. And then she kind of kept running away. Over and over again. ... And I just, like, waited for her. Like I didn't go to school, and I didn't make any friends and I didn't ... do anything. Because in my mind it was temporary. I thought she'd find whatever she was looking for.'

With their mother gone, Flick is now free. However, she isn't straining at the leash. Having done nothing with her life seems to almost be a point of pride, and it's tempting to wonder whether she found her mother's dependence convenient. As long as one is needed, one has a good excuse for putting any ambitions on hold.

Escape, stagnation, action, paralysis—these entwined strands run throughout the play. They find expression in theatrical imagery, from the 'festy' water of the swimming pool to the enforced lockdown; from

Declan's freezing up when he could be saving a life, to the elusive Mac, whistling as he wanders off 'looking for something better'. Bobbi rarely appears without carrying her caged 'wild rat'; at one point Flick refers to the baby's cot with, 'Why do you keep her in a cage?'

Bobbi is the only character who seems quite content with her circumstances (apart from her concern that her husband's been eaten by a croc). She doesn't yearn to leave the confines of Darwin or even of the Palms Motel. Unlike John, she isn't worried that she's not living her best life. She's a caretaker—not only in the managerial sense, but of those around her. Even while she's consumed with anxiety about Mac, she takes the time to bandage John's wound. In her opinion, the rat she finds roaming the streets needs rescuing—and perhaps she's right—but she ultimately comes to see that wild creatures don't belong in captivity, and releases it.

From the swarming chaos of these people's lives, a kind of strange calm ultimately descends on them. When they stop trying to control each other, when they give up trying to be what they're not, they are able to move on. The gate opens, the reptiles retreat, and it seems that even the most provocative of risks needn't end in carnage.

Early on, Renata justifies jumping the fence for a look at the crocodiles by saying that everything's chaos, 'The world's ending.'

> BOBBI: World's ending?
> RENATA: Yes. I think it is.
> BOBBI: Still here though. Not done yet. Still time to, you know, be a bit careful. Take care of everythin'. No point otherwise.
> RENATA: No point to what?
> BOBBI: Dunno do I? Being human.

If COVID-19 taught us anything, it's that we're all intricately connected. Selfique culture doesn't cut it. Nothing can survive, let alone thrive, in isolation. We depend on each other, and are affected by each other's actions. While we must grab the gift of being alive with both hands, we can't forget that, for good or ill, everything we do makes a difference.

Hilary Bell

Danny Ball in Belvoir 25A's Darwin's Reptilia, *2023 (Photo: Philip Erbarcher)*

Zoe Jensen in Belvoir 25A's Darwin's Reptilia, *2023 (Photo: Philip Erbarcher)*

Danny Ball and Zoe Jensen in Belvoir 25A's Darwin's Reptilia, *2023 (Photo: Philip Erbarcher)*

Darwin's Reptilia was first produced by JackRabbit Productions and premiered at downstairs Belvoir St Theatre, Gadigal country, Sydney, on 15 November, 2023, with the following cast:

RENATA	Ainslie McGlynn
DECLAN	Danny Ball
JOHN	Mathew Lee
BOBBI	Leilani Loau
FLICK	Zoe Jensen

Director, Samantha Young
Set and Costume Designer, Ruth Arnold
Lighting Designer, Saint Clair
Composition and Sound Designer, Hewett Cook
Stage Manager, Alex Liang
Dialect Coach, Alistair Toogood

CHARACTERS

RENATA, female, North American accent, thirties.
DECLAN, male, Galway accent, late thirties–early forties.
JOHN, male, North American accent, thirties.
BOBBI, female, Australian accent, late fifties–early sixties.
FLICK, female, Australian accent, twenties.

SETTING

The open-air pool area of the Palms Motel, a withered budget inn, tucked away in Darwin, Australia, about ten minutes from the city centre.

The humidity should be obvious; the sun beating down, flies in the air. A modest pool sits centred, bordered by a sparse arrangement of two to three deckchairs on each side, suggesting a place long forgotten by tourist crowds.

The stage should be designed with two crucial entrances/exits that lend themselves to the story's progression. One is purposed as a gateway that leads to an unseen small reception outhouse and the shrublands and mangroves beyond the motel's periphery.

The second exit leads to the implied motel's inner sanctum—the rooms and the motel office.

The prologue is set at a glitzy book publicity event in New York City, mirroring the layout of the Darwin setting but in the icy grip of New York's winter. The pool may be substituted as a table or bar, possibly adorned with the evening's promotional materials.

Lighting and soundscape serve to differentiate between the two polar settings, creating a tangible contrast between the dry solitude of Darwin and the feverish buzz of New York City.

TIME

December 2023

NOTES

A forward slash [/] indicates that the following line begins over the current one.

A dash [—] signifies interrupted speech.

Beats, pauses, and silences are indicated only as suggestions and are to be used at the director's discretion.

PROLOGUE

Winter, December in New York City.

A book publicity event, held at a publisher's modern apartment.

RENATA *and* DECLAN *have found refuge from the event's frenetic energy on an isolated outdoor terrace.*

We can hear the faint rumblings of the ongoing frivolities inside; writers mingling, glasses clinking, an air of pretension.

RENATA, *dressed for the cold but glamorous enough, stares down at the bustling Manhattan streets below.*

She is disarmingly still.

DECLAN, *uncomfortable in a suit, watches the inside goings-on with disdain.*

This opening moment lingers before any dialogue.

DECLAN: Smoke.
RENATA: What?
DECLAN: Hm?
RENATA: Smoke.
DECLAN: You see that / smoke?
RENATA: He's smoking.
DECLAN: Yer. He's inside, so, just—how do you know him again?
RENATA: That's Micah. I know Micah.
DECLAN: Yes. How do you know him?
RENATA: Micah?
DECLAN: … *Yes.*
RENATA: He published it. He's in publishing. And a writer. He writes about / things.
DECLAN: Don't like him. Obnoxious. Reminds me of—
RENATA: Of what?
DECLAN: Of smoking.
RENATA: You smoke though.

DECLAN: Ah? No. No I don't. What?
RENATA: What?
DECLAN: I don't do that. I tamed that beast.
RENATA: Okay.
DECLAN: Ah?
RENATA: I said okay. You don't smoke. I thought you did.
DECLAN: I quit, Ren. You didn't notice. Three weeks ago.

Pause.

What's the point of this thing? We're just standin' out—
RENATA: Look like little ants down there.
DECLAN: They're all laughin' in there. Look. What they laughin' at?
RENATA: Someone told a funny joke probably. They are noisy.
DECLAN: Feel odd just standin' here. Are they laughing at, like—you haven't really introduced me to anyone. Do you know that? Just *Micah.*
RENATA: You want to go back inside?
DECLAN: Well he's smoking.
RENATA: Just needed to show my face. You don't have to do anything.
DECLAN: Well then why did we come? Came out last year. Seems strange to have a party / now.
RENATA: It's publicity. So I can stay rich.
DECLAN: Everyone's read it already.
RENATA: You didn't read it.
DECLAN: Not fair, that. Got a reading problem.
RENATA: You can't read?
DECLAN: Like a concentration problem.
RENATA: Maybe I have that too.
DECLAN: Do you need to talk or make a speech or what? Not talking much. You don't want to / talk?
RENATA: I'm bored, Declan. You're boring me with this. Stop.
DECLAN: Nothin' wrong with borin'.
RENATA: You love boring, do you?
DECLAN: S'pose you think he's thrilling. An exciting little freak.
RENATA: Who?
DECLAN: Micah in there. Micah. The white pants and … Writer is he? Bit over-the-top, these writers, aren't they?

RENATA: You're standing really close to me Declan.
DECLAN: Didn't even look at me before, did he. Couldn't look me in the eye. Talkin' shit too. 'This is the most exciting time in the world', 'We're on the precipice of—' what did he call it?
RENATA: Selfique culture.
DECLAN: Selfique! *Selfique* culture. Fucken, what the fuck.
RENATA: You can go if you / want.
DECLAN: What does it even mean? I couldn't understand what he even meant.
RENATA: Just, you know—individualism or ... whatever. He likes capitalism. Freedom. He's a bit ... you know.
DECLAN: He likes money. Talks a lot about money.
RENATA: He sells a lot of books.
DECLAN: Cold too. Cold out here. It's really freezing. What time is it anyway? I mean, he's not really introducing you—is it because I'm here?
RENATA: He said it plays better if not too many people meet me. For mystique.
DECLAN: Weird thing to say.
RENATA: No it's not.
DECLAN: Really stupid thing to say. They must be suffocating in there. That smoke. Looks warm though.
RENATA: What do you think would happen if I spat off the balcony here?
DECLAN: Somethin' off about him. Talkin' like he thinks I'm ... He thinks I'm, what? Boring? Not hungry enough? Fucken. *Writers.*
RENATA: I'm a writer.
DECLAN: Well, self-help ... not that that's ... yer ... what does he write about?
RENATA: The collapse of the world. Trump. How bad Trump is. He writes about Trump all the time.

Beat.

DECLAN: But that's not what he seemed to—he was all excited about—
RENATA: He sells books, Declan.

Beat.

DECLAN: It is late. We should probably—Lily's probably—is she okay with your da? Your da seemed nice. Not sure how he lives here though. Chaos everywhere.

Renata's phone buzzes.

On the way over—you see that man eating out of the bin? Eating a chicken carcass right out of the bin. Bones and skin flying everywhere.

RENATA: Um.

DECLAN: I hate New York. I really actually hate it here, do you know that? Everyone *smokes*. They're all, you know, addicted to everything. Rushing around. Like the place is on fire. Like a freezing, dirty fire.

RENATA: Something quite strange has just happened.

DECLAN: Smoking. No sense of death. Dying from a sludge of charcoal ejaculate sliding down his lungs.

RENATA: I wish you'd listen to me for a moment.

DECLAN: What? The balcony?

RENATA: The balcony?

DECLAN: I think if you spat over the balcony, it would just land on someone, and they would panic. As they should. Everyone should panic.

RENATA: Someone's sent me a / message.

DECLAN: What if there's a pregnant woman in there, he's just smoking … sometimes you can't tell if someone's pregnant. Sometimes there's no … girth. I mean, we know that, don't we? No idea. Dangerous— what's wrong?

Beat.

Ren?

RENATA: I have a message.

DECLAN: Yer.

RENATA: On my phone.

DECLAN: Where else would it be?

RENATA: My mother died. I think the funeral's going to be in Australia.

DECLAN: Ah?

RENATA: Yeah.

DECLAN: What happened?

RENATA: My mother just died. In Australia. I have a message.

Beat.

DECLAN: I'm a little confused. When did that happen?
RENATA: I said. I received a message.
DECLAN: Like now?
RENATA: Yes. On my phone.
DECLAN: I know it's on your—Australia?
RENATA: My mother just died in Australia.
DECLAN: I didn't know your ma was living in Australia.
RENATA: She isn't. She's dead.
DECLAN: Well … when was the last time you spoke to 'er?
RENATA: A long … when I was fifteen maybe. I've never even been to Australia.
DECLAN: Right. So, you're not … like you're not that upset.
RENATA: She's dead.
DECLAN: I know she's—you can be quite inscrutable, you know. Do you know that you can be inscrutable sometimes?
RENATA: Yeah.
DECLAN: Who told you anyway? How did she die? Why are—
RENATA: My sister.
DECLAN: What sister—you have a whole family down there, do you?
RENATA: I don't know her, really. They both just … they're just from there.

    Beat.

It's kind of serious.
DECLAN: I know it's serious.

    Beat.

Well. You know. I am sorry. You / alright?
RENATA: I should go. I think she wants me to go. Maybe I'll just go. It could be fun. Maybe it'll be really fun.
DECLAN: Well hang on—what'd yer sister say?
RENATA: Half.
DECLAN: Half?
RENATA: She's my half-sister.
DECLAN: Well what is that?
RENATA: What do you mean what is that?
DECLAN: I just didn't know that. I didn't know any of this. I'm quite flabbergasted. I'm actually getting quite upset. Can you not … read me?

RENATA: It's not like I can't go. I have the time. I have the money.

DECLAN: That's not exactly right, I mean, we're meant to fly out tomorrow so we can't just … you'll feel better when we get there— Galway. Parents keen to meet yer. Meet Lily. Galway, huh?

RENATA: She didn't say when the funeral was. I imagine it would be soon. How far is it?

DECLAN: Galway?

RENATA: No.

DECLAN: I told Ma and Da we'll be home for Christmas. It sounds like you didn't know her, so. And we got Lil. We can't keep jumping all over the world every few months. You do this, you know. You like to leave when things get boring.

RENATA: Boring? My mother's dead.

DECLAN: I know Ren, but it's … I know.

> *Beat.*

Death is … confusing, and … The Grim Reaper and all. But we must remember, we got a baby now, ah? Have to think about it don't yer. Not just us anymore. Not just about you—

RENATA: I can't go to Australia because we have a baby?

DECLAN: You'd think he'd get a vape pen. Little vape / pen.

RENATA: If I did go, just for the funeral, you wouldn't have to come. Lily doesn't have to come. Might not be safe for her. They have these zebra-dog hybrid things, I think. Yes, they do. They run around killing little children.

DECLAN: Why would you tell me something like that?

RENATA: You don't have to come.

DECLAN: Well I can't stay in New *York*. With *Micah*.

RENATA: What? You don't live with Micah. What's wrong with you? You don't have to see Micah ever again. This is a party.

DECLAN: We have to do the tree. Da will be angry if we're not there for the tree.

RENATA: She lives in Darwin. My / sister.

DECLAN: The presents. Got to put the star on the top and / everything.

RENATA: Do you know Darwin?

DECLAN: Never heard of it. Sounds made up. I'm not taking this seriously, you're just in shock —

PROLOGUE

As the pair continue, JOHN *enters at the back of the stage, a copy of Renata's book in hand. He is nervous, eyes wide.*

Frozen with excitement as he clocks RENATA, *he waits for his moment, listening in.*

RENATA: It's a little city. At the top of Australia. It's not crazy. To go there, I mean. I want to go.

DECLAN: He's opening a window. Wants the smoke outside as well, does he?

RENATA: It'll be warm. It's always warm there. She wouldn't have sent me a message if she didn't want me / to go.

DECLAN: I need to calm / down.

RENATA: She's probably lonely.

DECLAN: I can't let this go on. Sick of standing by and just letting this continue.

RENATA: Then go and *do* something for once.

DECLAN *looks at her, makes the decision, and exits.*

JOHN, *anxious to introduce himself, slowly walks towards* RENATA.

He trips as he approaches.

JOHN: Heck.

RENATA: Oh.

JOHN: That was so, like, stupid. Can you believe I just about fell over here? God I could have hit my head. Died. That would be really just so fricken silly. I could have just died at this here party.

RENATA: At this here party.

JOHN: I was just, like, hanging out here. Yeah. Sometimes I just hang out, you know. I didn't mean to uh, overhear or anything. But um, are you like … you're going to Australia?

Beat. RENATA *stares him up and down.*

RENATA: Well, I do like Outback Steakhouse.

JOHN: Oh. Like. That's—that's like a funny joke. Heck. That's funny.

Beat. RENATA *clocks the book he's holding.*

Something changes in her.

RENATA: Yes. I am going to Australia.

JOHN: Gosh. I'd love that. I've never been anywhere. That's so crazy.
RENATA: You must really like it here.
JOHN: Oh. No. This country. It's doomed, do you know? Everything's crumbling, like, the world's ending. America. What if I don't get a chance to—like I almost just died at this party here, like *what*?
RENATA: I try not to think about / it.
JOHN: Like I've never travelled because I'm too anxious and I don't have much confidence, but I need to live life before we all run out of time. I'm getting old. Sometimes I just feel so old and boring and like, super weird. I'm not even that old.
RENATA: Everyone feels like that.
JOHN: And sometimes I'm on my phone and I read that all the ice is melting like a popsicle in a sauna and the animals are, like, playing this horrifying game of musical chairs. And soon *we're* going to be playing the musical chairs. And I don't want to play. And everyone *hates* each other. Everyone's piercing protest signs through each other's chests and screaming at the television and like, isn't Australia going to burn to death soon too? I read that. Didn't all the trees burn down? Aren't they all *fucked*?

    Pause.

RENATA: Well, the world must end at some point.
JOHN: You and your husband there—or your—you both look very nice, yeah. Very adult. I would've dressed up more, I didn't realise this was so um, conventional, or, proper.
RENATA: Conventional.
JOHN: No. I didn't / mean—
RENATA: I don't think I look conventional.
JOHN: Okay. No, I didn't mean you were like, plain or anything.
RENATA: He can smell blood.
JOHN: What?
RENATA: He can smell it. Blood. A tiny droplet from a mile away.

    Pause.

We went and got some soup once. We went to a soup place, and he got an orange soup. Probably pumpkin or—
JOHN: Or carrot.
RENATA: No. It wasn't carrot soup.

JOHN: Oh.

RENATA: He looks into the bowl, then looks up at me as if he were about to cry. Like a sad little dog. And he says they put blood in his soup. But I looked at it and I say to him, I say there's no blood in this soup, and he—Declan, his name is Declan—he says, oh really? Well somebody's bleeding. So then the chef walks by. The soup chef. And Declan seizes this poor man's collar, almost choking him to death, and he pulls him towards us and begins to scream like a tire screeching [*screaming*] 'WHERE'S THE BLOOD? WHERE'S THE BLOOD? I CAN SMELL IT!'

Beat.

The chef had a tiny cut on his finger. So I mean, I said okay? You were right? I guess there was a bit of blood in your soup?

Beat.

Anyway. Just saying. Not conventional.

Beat.

JOHN: 'There is no waiting for the perfect moment, no way to find stability and comfort, without the impulsive detours that we may find are our greatest strengths.'

RENATA: Oh.

JOHN: I read your book.

RENATA: Yes.

JOHN: My dad bought it for me, and I was like, okay Dad you big weirdo ... you big ... boomer weirdo. He thinks I have problems. He thinks I'm scared of everything. Because I don't have a relationship and I don't have much money, because of, like, the economy ... or any friends. And he's kinda dying, so I guess he thought a self-help book ... So I read it? Well just wow. It changed my life. Totally. Impulse is key, right? Live life by the gut, don't settle for anything. All the steps are so *clear* and the way you've kind of like, written about your own journey, you know?

Beat.

Like your wild life, the travelling and all the amazing people you've met and just the *freedom*. I've kind of had a stupid life. Sometimes I think that. Yeah. Trying to change. I'm doing them, the steps in

your book. I'm up to step eight. I quit my job, I'm moving out of my dad's apartment and just … starting over. Moving away from him and just all of that, um, boredom. And sadness. You know? So. Pretty good.
RENATA: Hm.

Beat.

JOHN: I'm John, also.
RENATA: Renata.
JOHN: Quigley.
RENATA: What?
JOHN: Quigley. My last name.
RENATA: You're going to leave your dying father?
JOHN: Well not like … just step eight. 'Cut Loose and Fly High.'
RENATA: Critical step.

Beat.

JOHN: Yeah …
RENATA: Well.
JOHN: I called your publisher to see if you were—he's the one who told me about this, so. Micah. Yeah. He actually said, you're working on a second book? Is that true? Are there going to be more steps?
RENATA: Yes. Of course.
JOHN: Amazing. *Yes.* So you'll write it in Australia? Gosh, well, lots of inspiration there. Did you know, and I read about this, apparently there are these demonic rats over there, in Australia. They call them devils. They have these feeding frenzies in the middle of the night, and they eat other animals whole, like they digest the fur and the bones and the nails and the teeth. When they feed. They can't help themselves. Imagine.
RENATA: I know about the devils. I've been to Australia. I've seen them.
JOHN: Of course. Of course, you've been there. You've been everywhere.
Like I said, I've barely left—
RENATA: Well maybe you should go. To Australia. Before we all die.
JOHN: Yes. Yes! I should! Oh, I'm just so excited there's another book. I was worried there wouldn't be any more steps—

Screams from the party.

PROLOGUE

DECLAN *enters suddenly, bloodstains on his outfit.*
He's out of breath, shock on his face, shaking.
Looking over his shoulder to the party, he walks to RENATA.
JOHN *is terrified, retreating a little.*
DECLAN *faces* RENATA, *ignoring* JOHN.

DECLAN: We have to leave. There's blood.
RENATA: Why is there blood?
DECLAN: Tiny fork—
RENATA: Tiny fork?
DECLAN: Oyster fork. Those forks for the oysters. They're not that big. He's not dying, he's just got a bit of a gash in his eye. We were only talking but he fell on to the fork, eye first. And I couldn't … didn't know what to do. I just, um—
RENATA: Did you help him? You should help him—
DECLAN: I couldn't help him. I hate this city, really. No place fit for a human. Shit everywhere. We need to / leave—
RENATA: Did they call an ambulance?
DECLAN: Who would know? They're all *busy* here. I just …

DECLAN *rushes to exit, muttering.*

RENATA: It was nice to meet you, John.
JOHN: Oh hey, meeting you so good. Love to meet you always and—nice—just—those new steps, when will the new steps be …

RENATA *is gone, following* DECLAN *offstage.*
Blackout.

ACT ONE

SCENE ONE

A few days later. Australian summer, December. Morning.

The open-air swimming area of The Palms Motel, Darwin, a cement oasis which seems to have absorbed and reflected a shimmering brightness.

Sun is beating down, flies are buzzing in the air.

FLICK lays sprawled on a deckchair.

She's sleeping, yet her eyes are disarmingly open. She's snoring.

A book, LIFE OFF LEASH: A Guide to Embracing Chaos, *lays abandoned by her side.*

Thrumming beats of metal music emanate from her oversized headphones.

Eventually, she rises, as if in a dream, sleepwalking, and approaches the pool, haphazardly grabbing the nearby book as she passes.

She stands, looking dead-eyed into the pool before abruptly submerging the book.

She returns to her deckchair, sleeping again.

After a moment, BOBBI *enters from the motel gate, holding a small cage, an air of mild distress.*

BOBBI: Oi.

> *Nothing.*

> BOBBI *exits into the motel doorway.*

[*Offstage*] Oi. Flick. You seen Mac?

> BOBBI *returns, cage still in hand.*

Flick. Oi, have you—Flick, you seen Mac?

> *After a beat of nothing,* BOBBI *walks to the pool and cups some water in her hands. She throws it in* FLICK*'s face.*

FLICK: [*sputtering*] The *fuck*—
BOBBI: Where the / keys?
FLICK: You got piss water on my—I was / sleeping.
BOBBI: Where the keys for that / gate?
FLICK: Got 'em in my room. Trying to / relax.
BOBBI: You need to keep 'em out—you see what they're doin' / out there?
FLICK: You look a bit wobbly. You right?

>BOBBI *looks out in search.*

BOBBI: About to shut down the roads. I need to find Mac, he / keeps—
FLICK: What roads?
BOBBI: The roads, Flick. There are roads—
FLICK: I know the roads. Roads everywhere.
BOBBI: He'll only have an hour I reckon before they shut and / that.
FLICK: What they shutting down for? And what's that?
BOBBI: It's a rat, I found a rat. Thought I'd save her didn't I, yes I did.
FLICK: You saved a / rat.
BOBBI: Crocodiles all up and down the roads. They're locking it all up, aren't they.
FLICK: Serious?
BOBBI: Somethin' strange goin' on …

>BOBBI *takes a breath.*

>Crocs down in the scrubland there. A lot of 'em. They've just eaten two Swedes.

FLICK: Nah.
BOBBI: Yeah.
FLICK: Don't think so.
BOBBI: Tellin' you.
FLICK: Two Swedes?
BOBBI: Swedes isn't the point, didn't meant to say Swedes, but—
FLICK: Said it but.
BOBBI: They're Swedish.
FLICK: Yeah?
BOBBI: There are crocodiles everywhere—
FLICK: Serious?
BOBBI: Need to tell Mac.

FLICK: Might be gettin' his dick wet / again.
BOBBI: *Flick*, that's not on.
FLICK: Chasing tail again I / bet.
BOBBI: Cops all down the highway. Even in town, reckon they're headin' on to Mitchell and the lagoon and that. Grab those keys and lock the gate out there, would you?
FLICK: I just woke up—
BOBBI: *Flick*, c'mon.
FLICK: [*exiting*] Well what's happened?
BOBBI: Need to cancel bookings. They're about to close up everything this side of the highway. Cops outside tellin' everyone to stay in. I even saw one. They're all over, darls. Reckon we won't be allowed out for a few days.

    FLICK *re-enters holding the keys.*

FLICK: Fuck off.
BOBBI: Fuck *you*.
FLICK: What about like Christmas and bookings and all that?
BOBBI: Flick, *please* just go and lock the gate. And leave them keys under the mat for Mac.
FLICK: Fine.

    FLICK *exits to lock the gate.*

BOBBI: [*under her breath, perhaps to the rat*] Could be a strange Christmas. But he'll be back. Probably just a quick walk out there hey?

    Pause.

FLICK: [*re-entering*] So like, well what about—like what about money?
BOBBI: Dunno, do I? Got a motel with no guests. Hopefully only a few days. Wish Mac was here, he'd —he'd know what to do.
FLICK: Mac wouldn't do shit.
BOBBI: Why you always goin' at him?

    Beat. BOBBI *sits on a deckchair, a little exhausted.*

FLICK: Wow. So. Kind of exciting.
BOBBI: Not exciting. Crocs eatin' Swedes all over the place.
FLICK: Nah but just, good story one day.
BOBBI: Good story for who?

FLICK: Just a good story. Tell at the pub or, write a book about it or somethin'. Crocodiles everywhere. Make a movie. Never have any stories.
BOBBI: What do rats eat?
FLICK: What're you gonna do with that?
BOBBI: I dunno. Take care of her.
FLICK: It's meant to be running around.
BOBBI: How long you been sleepin' for? You didn't hear Mac's whistle, did ya?
FLICK: I was listening to music.
BOBBI: He'll be back. Always comes back.
FLICK: Yeah.
BOBBI: Yeah what?
FLICK: Just sayin' … yeah.
BOBBI: Rosie. I'll her call her Rosie.
FLICK: Could've sworn I saw some people out there. Comin' up this way.
BOBBI: You what?
RENATA: [*offstage*] Hello?

Pause.

BOBBI: You didn't lock it.
FLICK: Could've sworn—
BOBBI: Christ—
FLICK: You got a booking or somethin'?
BOBBI: There was nothin' today.
FLICK: Do I smell?
BOBBI: I'm used to it.

>RENATA *and* DECLAN *enter from the motel gate.*
>
>DECLAN*'s wearing thick dark sunglasses and a baby-wrap holding the child.*
>
>RENATA, *also wearing thick sunglasses, lugs a suitcase.*
>
>*They look like New York.*
>
>FLICK *is shocked. She sniffs her armpits.*

RENATA: There was no-one at reception. Sorry, we found these keys in the gate—
DECLAN: You should have a bell. You can buy these little bells. Probably cheap. Strange you don't have / one.

BOBBI: I'm sorry you—do you have a booking—I'm sorry dear—Flick you can't be leavin' those keys in the bloody gate ...

>BOBBI *takes the keys and exits.*

FLICK: Whoa.
RENATA: Hello.
FLICK: Hi. Renata?
RENATA: Hi Felicity.

>BOBBI *re-enters.*

BOBBI: Sorry miss, you seen the news? We're not taking any guests—there's a bit of a crisis—
FLICK: Fuck, man.
BOBBI: Clean your mouth out Flick—
FLICK: It's my—uh—this is my sister.
RENATA: Surprise.
DECLAN: Surprise.

>FLICK *is shocked, but emotions are there.*
>
>*After a beat, they awkwardly hug.*
>
>*As they do,* DECLAN *and* BOBBI *stand awkwardly.*

I'd hug you, but I have a baby strapped to my chest.

>*Beat.*

That's not like a joke. I'm a father. This is a real baby.
BOBBI: I'm Bobbi.
DECLAN: Like Bob? Like Robert?
BOBBI: [*to* RENATA] Flick's told me so much about you—
FLICK: Didn't say that much. What are you talking / about?
RENATA: This is Declan. He's—yeah. This is Declan.
DECLAN: Yer.
BOBBI: I mean you said a little bit about / her.
FLICK: Can you shut / up?
RENATA: You're allowed to talk about me.
DECLAN: You can talk about me too.
RENATA: Declan.
FLICK: I didn't know you were—I had no idea you were coming—
DECLAN: Somethin' happenin' out / there?

ACT ONE 17

BOBBI: Can I get you some / water?
RENATA: Well I thought we should be here for the funeral.
DECLAN: Water would be / nice.
BOBBI: You're havin' a funeral?
RENATA: You sent me a message.
DECLAN: There's kind of like a big hullabaloo out / there.
FLICK: Yeah, but, you should have told me, because there's—
RENATA: I thought the surprise might be nice. Surprises are good. Even with death.
DECLAN: Surprise death. Always / good.
FLICK: Oh. Yeah. No it is. And you have a baby.
RENATA: Yes. I didn't want one. I wasn't trying to have one, I mean.

Beat.

We didn't even really know each / other.
DECLAN: We did know each / other.
RENATA: I actually didn't even know I was pregnant until it was too late to … yeah.

Beat.

Is that a rat?
BOBBI: Found 'er. Needs some lovin' I reckon, yes I do, don't I? Yes.
RENATA: That's a wild rat?
BOBBI: Yes.
RENATA: You don't think it needs to run around?
BOBBI: Ah?
RENATA: It's wild.
BOBBI: Yeah but she's alright. Gave her a name and everythin'. Rosie. Little Rosie. No good?

Beat.

RENATA: We saw cops. There are cops all down the road. It's like—
DECLAN: It's like hell.
BOBBI: Yes / well—
RENATA: It's not like hell, it's just / different.
BOBBI: Crocodiles. There are these things here, in Darwin, they're called crocodiles. They look quite cute. Quite tempting to give 'em a little pat, but they've kind of invaded a little more than we're used

to today. The mangroves have become a bit, um, withered darls, oh yeah, yes, so they can't live there, they're / withered—
FLICK: Mangroves are all fucked—
BOBBI: —so they're comin' in, the crocs, and well I don't think we're going to be allowed outside for a bit. Until they sort it.
RENATA: That's incredible.
DECLAN: Certainly worth the root-canal of a plane ride / over.
BOBBI: Don't s'pose you saw a man on your way in? Handsome bloke, no hair, beer belly, whistling—he's always whistling—
RENATA: We didn't see anyone. Just / cops.
DECLAN: Would really love some / water.
BOBBI: Always getting into trouble he is. My man. Yeah. So. Yeah. No. Think he just went for a walk. A look. Lookin' for somethin' better! No, only joking, only joking. Maybe though.

Pause.

What's the doll's name?
DECLAN: Lily.
BOBBI: Beautiful name that is, oh yeah, a real beauty. Like the flower.
RENATA: I'm still not sure about it.
FLICK: You can stay though. Yeah. There's like a room and everything. I just didn't know you were … but I guess no-one's coming now anyway.
BOBBI: Gotta cancel those bookings.
FLICK: It's just us. For as long as / you want.
DECLAN: Well I feel like we should maybe leave.
BOBBI: We can talk money later.
FLICK: Bobbi, she's not going to pay the—she's famous.
RENATA: We'll pay. Famous people have money.
BOBBI: Oh yes, the *book*, the book, very happy for / you.
DECLAN: I mean are we allowed to leave?
RENATA: [*to* FLICK] It's good to meet you. In person finally. And I'm sorry about your mother.
FLICK: Yeah. Same. Like. Sorry to you. About Mum.
BOBBI: Oh yeah, yeah.
DECLAN: Yer.

Pause.

RENATA: I tried to call you. From the airport.

FLICK: Oh, I was sleeping.
BOBBI: She has narcopepsi.
FLICK: That's not the word.
DECLAN: It's narcolepsy.
BOBBI: Narcolepsy.
FLICK: No.
DECLAN: It's not narcolepsy?
BOBBI: It is narcolepsy.
DECLAN: Fuck?
FLICK: I don't have … well I don't know. I just sleep sometimes.
BOBBI: All the time.
RENATA: When's the funeral?
FLICK: Oh. Don't worry about that. I did my own thing. Yeah. That's all fine.
RENATA: You did your own funeral?
FLICK: She didn't want a funeral so I just, like, threw some flowers around. Lilies, actually.
RENATA: You threw some flowers / around?
BOBBI: Where'd you do / that?
RENATA: There's no funeral?
DECLAN: Brilliant.
FLICK: You flew here for the funeral?
RENATA: I just didn't know there wasn't going to be a funeral.
FLICK: Well you didn't tell me you were, like, coming here.
RENATA: No.
FLICK: No.
RENATA: Well I thought I could help. If I had known about the flowers. I could have helped.
DECLAN: Helped throw some flowers around?
RENATA: Beaches look nice.
BOBBI: You can't go to the beach.

Beat.

RENATA: Is that my book?
FLICK: Oh. Yeah.
RENATA: It's wet.

Fade to black.

SCENE TWO

Afternoon. RENATA *and* FLICK *laze on deckchairs.* FLICK *sits upright, watching* RENATA *with curiosity.* RENATA *faces out towards the expanse beyond the pool gate, oblivious to* FLICK*'s stare.*

Silence lingers, the air taut with expectation as FLICK *contemplates bridging the gap of conversation.*

FLICK: Do you like metal?
RENATA: Hm?
FLICK: Metal music. Heavy metal.
RENATA: What's out there?
FLICK: It's the mangroves. Like bush … with water? You know what bush is. And then the highway.
RENATA: Yeah.
FLICK: Two Swedes got eaten just down there. From Sweden.

    Beat.

You're kind of not what I thought you'd be like.
RENATA: Everyone says that.
FLICK: Just kinda not what I thought. You're pretty. But I knew that. I saw photos and an interview and yeah.
RENATA: Why didn't your mother—
FLICK: I heard you on that podcast. That NPR one. Or the *New York Times*—I can't remember—you got interviewed.
RENATA: You listen to NPR here?
FLICK: Well anyone can listen to NPR.
RENATA: No. I know.
FLICK: It's on the internet. We have the internet.
RENATA: Yes.
FLICK: That was a good interview. You were like, really loud, huh. And you were pretty funny too. I thought … hah … that's funny. What's her name—that woman, who did the interview— Jenny. No, Gerrie. No, Terry? Yeah. I thought she was rude to you, like kind of saying you were a liar and 'blah blah don't you *care* about *responsibility*?' and you, like, yelled. Didn't you? You yelled at Terry. You called her a cunt.

RENATA: I was on cocaine.

Beat.

FLICK: Do you take a lot of / drugs?
RENATA: And your mother stayed here?
FLICK: Sometimes. She was here sometimes.
RENATA: What did she do?
FLICK: Odd jobs. She would clean the pool sometimes. It's pissy.
RENATA: It's pissy.
FLICK: Yeah it's festy.
RENATA: What did she do all day?
FLICK: What do you mean?
RENATA: I mean what did she do?
FLICK: Um. Well. There's heaps to do here. Like usually. Not when there's … There are nice beaches. You can't swim in them a lot of the time. But that's okay. And the lagoon, pretty nice. But people shit in there all the time. There's just like, always shit in there. So I don't go in there. With the shit. There's like a wave pool? On Kitchener? You seen that?
RENATA: I haven't left the motel.

Beat.

FLICK: It has fake waves. It's fun. But it's probably not as good compared to … what's that place … with the big waves?
RENATA: Hawaii.
FLICK: No, in America.
RENATA: That's in America.
FLICK: Nah—
RENATA: Yes.

Pause.

FLICK: The wave pool is cool. And someone's always there to help you if you get a bit stressed out, because it's always packed, it can get chaotic. Like, Bobbi came with me once and she got fucken hit in the face by this big inflatable duck. This Brazilian guy, he was on an inflatable fucken duck, and it went flying and it just skull-fucked her.

Beat.

RENATA: That's a great story.

FLICK: Thank you. Yeah. It's pretty crazy here. But they are fake. The waves.

RENATA: How long do these crocodile things normally go for? What's everyone meant to do?

FLICK: I don't think this has happened before.

RENATA: You'd think they could round 'em all up and just shoot them or something. Stitch together some meat and throw it somewhere and wait for them to come. Throw it in the town square.

FLICK: Town square?

RENATA: Is there a town square?

FLICK: Smith Street Mall. We have that. It gets buzzy on the weekends.

RENATA: They should just get rid of them.

FLICK: Well you can't just kill all the crocodiles.

RENATA: Why not?

FLICK: Just shouldn't. Not their fault they got nowhere to go. Mangroves are all fucked.

RENATA: Just seems like there's an easy solution.

FLICK: Let it burn, huh?

RENATA: Excuse me?

FLICK: Mum used to say that. Let it burn! Like if she thought there was an easy way out. Mum used to camp a lot, like whenever she was kind of running away—

RENATA: Running from / what?

FLICK: Nah just like, she was always on the move. And she would camp and set up these tents and then she'd get bored and want to come here or whatever so she'd just, like, burn the whole thing? Like burn the tent and everything inside and just come back? Like it never happened. Just leave all her burnt shit in the bush.

    RENATA *is laughing a bit.*

RENATA: I like that. Let it burn.

FLICK: She'd come back smelling like smoke with these stories, like she had to leave the campsite because a ranger was stalking her, or she'd been having some affair with a serial killer who was hiding out in the mangroves, or she'd seen an alien. None of them were real.

RENATA: What do you mean?

ACT ONE

FLICK: You just knew. She was lying. You just knew with her.

Beat.

Do you like New / York—

RENATA: How did she die anyway? You didn't say much in your message.

FLICK: Oh. She like … she just kinda died. She was unwell, yeah. Mentally. Just uh, couldn't take care of herself I guess. Maybe she had a brain tumour or something.

RENATA: Did anyone check to see if she had a brain / tumour?

FLICK: I didn't mean she actually had a brain tumour. Just, she acted like maybe she did.

Beat.

Anyway. It's really pretty good here. You just came at a bad time. Like, I didn't know you were coming. So yeah. I would have planned something.

RENATA: Why didn't she want a funeral?

FLICK: I don't know.

Beat.

I don't know how to— I'm sorry like, she left you. When you were young. Mum yeah, said she loved you, so. Heard her say that. Just if that's like, what you needed to hear. That's why I said that. If that's why you came. So. Pretty good.

RENATA: That is pretty good.

Beat.

FLICK: You're kinda funny.

RENATA: Am I? Was she funny?

FLICK: Sometimes, yeah. When she relaxed. You would have gotten along I reckon.

RENATA: I think it's good I came here. I should have done it sooner. When I was younger maybe. Without a baby.

FLICK: You kinda don't seem like you have a baby anyway.

RENATA: Thank you.

Beat.

FLICK: She was proud of you as well. With the book. And … same.

Beat. RENATA *smiles.*

RENATA: You know? I actually wasn't on cocaine. In that interview. I don't even know why I said that.
FLICK: What?
RENATA: Yeah I just said that. I don't know.

Beat.

FLICK: That's silly.
RENATA: It is silly.
FLICK: That's so stupid.

They laugh.

A crocodile rumbles.

FLICK *and* RENATA *turn towards the mangroves over the gate.*

There you go. A real live one.
RENATA: Oh my … Felicity.
FLICK: Yeah.
RENATA: Hm.
FLICK: What?
RENATA: It looks happy.

Fade to black.

SCENE THREE

Early evening. DECLAN *is perched uncomfortably on a deckchair, skin glistening from sweat.* BOBBI *enters with her rat, watching* DECLAN *as he wrestles with discomfort. As she pauses to light a cigarette,* BOBBI's *eyes remain on* DECLAN, *fascinated by his struggle with the harsh conditions. Suddenly,* DECLAN *raises his head, catching the scent of the cigarette smoke.*

BOBBI: Ay.
DECLAN: Alright Bobbi.
BOBBI: You right?
DECLAN: Yer. Fine.
BOBBI: Not used to the heat.
DECLAN: Not really.
BOBBI: How's the bub?

ACT ONE

DECLAN: She's in the room with—you smokin'?
BOBBI: You want one?
DECLAN: No. I quit. I quit actually. Almost four weeks ago.
BOBBI: Why you quit?
DECLAN: Have a child. So. Trying not to die. Would you mind—
BOBBI: Did you open this gate? Swear I locked it ...

> BOBBI *exits to the gate.*

DECLAN: Not sure the gate's well-equipped there, Bobbi. They can slip through them bars there, no?
BOBBI: [*offstage*] Just needs to stay / closed.
DECLAN: I mean if we can see them, they can see us, no?

> BOBBI *re-enters.*

Not good for babies either. Did you know that? The smoke. Gets in their faces and they grow up blind.
BOBBI: Blind?
DECLAN: And deaf. They go deaf too. They go deaf and blind. Not good for the rat either. Don't want a deaf rat, do you?

> BOBBI *blows smoke.*

Just looking after my family. It'd be good not to have smoke around / 'em.
BOBBI: Well your family's in the other—
DECLAN: I know where my family is. They're in the other room. I know that. I'm just sayin'.

> *Beat.*

BOBBI: Still can't find him. My Mac. He does this. Goes out when he shouldn't. You haven't heard him whistling? He whistles up a storm doesn't he. Sounds like a giant recorder. Not the only giant recorder he's got either if you know what I mean hah! No, no only joking. But yes he does. Whistle.
DECLAN: Right.
BOBBI: You know some people, they can't sit still, can they? And I tell him, I say mate you got it pretty good here, wakin' up in sunshine, relax by the pool, nothin' to worry about, good life and that. But he keeps goin' out. Sometimes it's not enough for people hey?
DECLAN: No, I guess it's not.

BOBBI: No, it's not, is it? No, it isn't.
DECLAN: No.

> *Beat.*

BOBBI: Don't know what he's lookin' for.
DECLAN: You ever been to Galway?
BOBBI: Never been anywhere.
DECLAN: Mm. Well it's a real … Do you know when we can leave yet?
BOBBI: You can't leave. Cops said.
DECLAN: No, I know. But when do you / think—
BOBBI: Not allowed out for a bit. They said.
DECLAN: I'm asking you—
BOBBI: Shh …

> BOBBI *stands, moves towards the gate.*

Something down there I think. Someone moving … you see that? [*Yelling*] Mac? … Mackenzie?

> *Suddenly,* RENATA *enters, having jumped over the motel gate.*
>
> *She's out of breath, as if she's been running, a wild smile on her face.*

What in the world—
DECLAN: The fuck are yer—

> RENATA *pulls* DECLAN *in and kisses him with passion and adrenalin.*
>
> *He kisses her back, the pair transported somewhere else for a moment.*
>
> BOBBI *watches on.*

[*Pulling away*] Ren—what—where's Lily?
RENATA: You start walking five minutes from here and it's chaos. Really, it's wild. I'm drenched in sweat. Look at me! Hah. Feels good. It's really—it's just / *wild.*
DECLAN: Where's Lily?
BOBBI: You cut yourself, darls?
DECLAN: Where *is* she?
RENATA: She's fine, she's sleeping in the room. I went for a walk. Just needed to—
DECLAN: She's alone?
RENATA: She was sleeping.

DECLAN: You just left her?
RENATA: It was just a walk.
DECLAN: Are you thinkin' straight?
BOBBI: Really shouldn't be going out / darl—
DECLAN: You're bleedin'. Clean that up Ren. Clean it up / now.
RENATA: It's a scratch, Declan.
BOBBI: Probably have a / Band-Aid somewhere or—
DECLAN: Losin' your mind / Ren.
BOBBI: Anti-sceptic
RENATA: I just felt like it. Just got the impulse. It's fine.
DECLAN: Can't just do things because you *feel* like it.
RENATA: I saw one. I've always wanted to see one. And I saw one.
BOBBI: Blood attracts them, darls.
RENATA: I think that's sharks.
BOBBI: Think I'd know.
RENATA: It smiled. Like it was an old friend.
DECLAN: It didn't smile Renata.
BOBBI: You really shouldn't be going out there darls, honestly they're unpredictable.
DECLAN: This is not a playground. It's not a zoo. Left our baby in the fucken room. It's crazy. Why are we in this shithole? There's no funeral, we're told we can't leave, and now yer hunting crocodiles are yer? We need to go home. We have to put the fucken star on the tree. This is *chaos*.
RENATA: Everything's chaos Declan. The world's ending.
DECLAN: The world is not ending Renata. Grow up. And clean up the blood. Please.

>*Beat.*
>
>DECLAN *retreats to the motel doorway.*

I'm going to go and look after our daughter.

>*He exits.*

BOBBI: Can't be doin' that, darls.
RENATA: He's just scared.
BOBBI: World's ending?
RENATA: Yes. I think it is.

BOBBI: Still here though. Not done yet. Still time to, you know, be a bit careful. Take care of everythin'. No point otherwise.
RENATA: No point to what?
BOBBI: Dunno, do I? Being human.

> *Beat*

You see my Mac out there?
RENATA: No. I didn't see him.
BOBBI: Be careful, darls.

> RENATA *exits.*
>
> *The low, guttural rumble of a crocodile is heard.*
>
> BOBBI *finishes her cigarette.*
>
> *Fade to black.*

SCENE FOUR

In the heat of the morning, the same open-air pool area.

RENATA *and* FLICK *lounge leisurely in their deckchairs on either side of the pool. The pair are engaged in a game of Two Truths and a Lie, both behind dark sunglasses.*

FLICK: Mum had a dog. Flash. One day, we're walking through Litchfield and this feral cat started to bite the shit out of his face, so I picked up a stick and I stabbed the cat in its eye, and it died.
RENATA: Hm. I don't know.
FLICK: I'm a certified deep-water diver.
RENATA: Okay.
FLICK: I've never left Darwin, and I never will leave Darwin. Not for my whole life.

> *Beat.*

RENATA: Why would you say that? You'll leave Darwin.
FLICK: That's not the game. You have to pick the lie. You have to pick one.
RENATA: That one. You're going to leave Darwin. One day.
FLICK: Wrong. I'm not a deep-water diver. I don't even *swim*.
RENATA: That's not—I don't get this game. How can you know you'll never leave—

FLICK: Get over it, you lost! Now go.

RENATA: You don't swim?

FLICK: Go!

RENATA: Okay. Okay okay ... hm ... I once had a threesome in a public street in Mexico City.

FLICK: Uh.

RENATA: What.

FLICK: Nothing.

RENATA: Okay. Charlotte Gainsbourg—do you know who—you know her—she cooked me dinner once. I met her at a party and she invited me for dinner. I told her a story, this thing I went through in Norway—long story—I basically went off-grid for a year. No electricity, no internet. Just the wilderness. So, I told her, and she pitched it to Netflix, as a film, you know. It got greenlit. My name's not on it. So, you know. She stole it from me.

FLICK: Right. Yeah. What's it called?

RENATA: What?

FLICK: What's the movie called?

RENATA: I think it's *Circle ... Circle* something? It's not out yet.

FLICK: I don't know who Charlotte Gainsbourg is.

Beat.

RENATA: I've never cried in my whole life. Neither has Declan.

FLICK: You've never—

RENATA: Yeah.

FLICK: That's a lie. You've cried. Declan's cried. C'mon. Lie.

RENATA: Wrong.

FLICK: Okay, well which one's the lie?

RENATA: They're all kind of true now that I think about it.

FLICK: They're not.

RENATA: Excuse me?

Beat.

FLICK: That's just not how you play the / game.

RENATA: It's boring anyway.

Beat.

Declan doesn't cry. He's sensitive, but he doesn't cry.

FLICK: Sensitive to what?
RENATA: Well—
FLICK: My B.O.?
RENATA: No. What?
FLICK: You can tell me if he said something. I've got like a fucken problem.
RENATA: I think you smell / fine.
FLICK: I stink so much. I put on all these different soaps and oils and shit. Mum put bleach under my armpits because she thought it would take the smell away but it just hurt.
RENATA: Why on earth did she do that?
FLICK: She wanted me to like, I don't know, meet someone.
RENATA: That's funny. She sounds funny.
FLICK: It wasn't that funny. Kind of cruel.

   Beat.

RENATA: I was at this crazy party last week, for my book. It was the most insane party I've ever been to. Everyone was there. And this guy, huge publisher guy, he was smoking, and Declan stabbed him in the—

   RENATA *stops and looks at* FLICK, *who—despite her eyes being slightly open—has fallen asleep.*

Flick. *Flick.*

   RENATA *shakes* FLICK.

   FLICK *wakes up.*

FLICK: Hi.
RENATA: Were you sleeping?
FLICK: Sorry. Must've just …
RENATA: Your eyes were open.
FLICK: Sorry.

   Beat.

RENATA: Right. Okay.
FLICK: What were we—Declan … Declan's …
RENATA: He can smell blood. He can smell it from a mile away.
FLICK: Oh. What?

   DECLAN *enters, sweaty. He's holding the baby cot and his phone.*

DECLAN: Ma and Da say hi, Ren.

RENATA: Hi.
DECLAN: Told 'em we're sticking to the weekend flight so we should—
FLICK: Hi.

> DECLAN *nods, confused.*

DECLAN: Yer. Hi.
FLICK: Why do you keep her in a cage?
RENATA: It's not a cage.
FLICK: Isn't it hot in there for her?
DECLAN: [*to* RENATA] Do you think it's too hot?
RENATA: Hot everywhere.
FLICK: You should give her some air.
DECLAN: Like outside air? Like what I'm doing right now?

> *Beat.*

Do you know if we can leave soon? Who do I ask? Is there like a reptile specialist or somethin'? Is there someone who like … manages … the town? It's almost Christmas.
RENATA: Can't miss an Irish Christmas.
FLICK: They might be gone before / Christmas.
DECLAN: Who told you that?
FLICK: You might be able to go to the wave pool.
RENATA: Well I simply must stay for the wave pool.
FLICK: Miss Hartford, I shall show you the wave pool.
DECLAN: Say wave pool again—
RENATA: [*simultaneous*] Wave pool.
FLICK: [*simultaneous*] Wave pool.

> *They smile.* DECLAN *doesn't.*
>
> *He stands, lifts the cot on his way.*

DECLAN: It's too hot. I'll take 'er inside.
RENATA: Yep.

> DECLAN *exits.*
>
> *Beat.*

FLICK: Sorry I fell asleep.
RENATA: Yeah.
FLICK: How did you guys meet?

RENATA: We met at San Fermin.
FLICK: What is that?
RENATA: You know San Fermin. The running of the bulls. In Pamplona. We were running with the bulls. I fell and he picked me up and then we kept running with them. It was my birthday.
FLICK: Twelfth of July.
RENATA: You … yeah. It was fun. It was hot. We were uncontrollable together. He was crazy.
FLICK: Wow.
RENATA: I know.

Beat.

FLICK: Bobbi told me you went out the other night.
RENATA: Bit of a gossip, isn't she.
FLICK: Kinda dangerous. Those Swedes died and everything.
RENATA: People die all the time.
FLICK: Still dangerous though. Got a baby now. Gotta be careful.
RENATA: She could die from anything too. Cot death.

Beat.

We should have a party.
FLICK: Here? With who?
RENATA: Yes. Whoever. Friends.
FLICK: I've never had a party.
RENATA: Course you haven't. It's easy. It's really easy. I can organise it. A Christmas party.
FLICK: Aren't you meant to go home by—
RENATA: Your mother never had parties?
FLICK: She did. But they were bad. Like fights and drug binges and police and—
RENATA: Sounds like a fun party.
FLICK: They weren't that fun.
RENATA: I'm sure she had fun.

Beat.

How did you know when my birthday is?
FLICK: It's in your book.

Beat.

And those stories you told me were also from the book. Charlotte Gainsbourg, the threesome in Mexico. They're from the book. Aren't they?

RENATA: So you do know who Charlotte Gainsbourg is.

FLICK: Not really. I just looked her up after I read it.

RENATA: You drowned the book, so I wasn't sure if you'd read / it.

FLICK: Oh. No, I was sleepwalking—must've dropped it in. I did read the book. I'm not like, doing your steps or whatever, but I remember all the stories.

RENATA: Don't take it too seriously.

FLICK: Didn't take it seriously.

RENATA: Okay. So.

FLICK: No I didn't mean—sorry, I just thought like, it was weird reading it. You've been to Madagascar and Vanuatu and Greece and everywhere and we were just never on the itinerary. Ever.

RENATA: It's far. Australia is far.

FLICK: But you came here now.

RENATA: Because your mother died, Felicity.

FLICK: But you never came when she was alive.

RENATA: Well she left me. I was a child. Wasn't going to come crawling back.

FLICK: Right.

RENATA: It's fine to think the book's bullshit. But it might be helpful. You've never left Darwin, so. Might be good to read it / again.

FLICK: What does that mean?

RENATA: Nothing. People find it helpful.

FLICK: I stayed here to look after Mum.

RENATA: Yeah but she's dead now.

FLICK: You would have stayed if you knew her.

RENATA: Don't you ever feel an innate desire to do something? Your own thing?

FLICK: Well yes. But I don't have the same life you have—

RENATA: That's your choice though. Which I don't get. I don't get that. The book says, you know, your own impulses and desires are quite shattering if you don't fulfill them—

FLICK: Do you have fulfillment?

RENATA: Yes. Yes I do. God it's hot. Aren't you hot? Maybe you do smell a little.

FLICK: Oh.

RENATA: Heat is suffocating.

FLICK: Well yeah, that's why I thought the baby might want some air—

RENATA: Shut up about the baby.

Pause.

Sorry. Let's go for a walk.

FLICK: We can't go for a walk.

RENATA: You're not listening to me.

FLICK: Whole world is listening to you. You wrote a book. Fucken famous.

RENATA: But you don't … they just don't quite get it.

A plane flies overhead.

Are people still coming here?

Beat. They watch the plane.

Why would anyone come here?

Beat.

I'm writing a new book. About this. About Darwin.

Beat.

We should go and do something.

Pause.

FLICK: Maybe I will have a party. It's my birthday on Saturday.

Fade to black.

SCENE FIVE

Evening. FLICK *is reclined on a deckchair, eyes open and sleeping.*

In the dim light, she rises, quietly humming as she aimlessly wonders around the pool's perimeter. The low, guttural rumble of a crocodile is heard.

DECLAN *emerges from the motel doorway, beer in hand. He pops a cigarette between his lips before rolling his eyes at the sight of* FLICK, *his chance at a solitary smoke gone awry.*

Struck by an impulse, FLICK *stands and submerges the set of keys into the pool's surface, her vacant gaze set towards the distant mangroves.*

DECLAN: Felicity?

>FLICK *continues staring.*

>DECLAN'S *unaware, but she's sleepwalking.*

Yer alright? There something in the water there?

>DECLAN *walks to the pool and stands beside* FLICK.

>FLICK *suddenly moves and takes her position back on a deckchair.*

If I were rude earlier. You know. Sorry. Irish.

>*Beat.*

Do you think ... I know you've been speakin' to Ren and all. Think she's a bit out of sorts or somethin'. I don't know.

>*Beat.*

To be honest with yer, I do sometimes feel ... well I feel like I could just be anyone, yer know? She needs to have someone, anyone, to watch her ... do whatever she does. So I'm just here. Like a ghost. Like she doesn't know me, sometimes, yer? But she's got it good, doesn't she? Got a baby. Forgets sometimes. Kind of annoyin', to be honest, that she doesn't get that. We got this thing here, this little potential organism and it's like she thinks it's just a pet, like a wee mouse, or a rat, or a fish, or somethin' ... hamster ... like it's temporary. Learnin' to be patient, but yer know ...

>DECLAN *spots the keys in the pool.*

>*He fishes them out.*

What're these ... these yours?

>*Beat.*

She seems to be liking you a lot. Talks about yer. Thinks yer fascinating. Wants to help you and everythin'. Maybe you'd have a word with her? She might listen to yer. Not askin' much, just ...

>DECLAN *holds his hand out to return the keys but is distracted by a whistling in the distance. He looks out beyond the gate, spotting movement in the bushes.*

You see that, Felicity?

Beat.

Somethin' out there I think … I think … I think … Christ, there's a man out there. What's he … Mate, what're you doin'? You tryna to get in? Or …

DECLAN's eyes are suddenly drawn to a large crocodile approaching the man from behind.

FUCK. FUCKEN—JUMP THE GATE! WHAT'RE YOU DOIN' MAN?

JUMP THE FUCKING GATE. I … I … I CAN'T HELP YER IF YOU DON'T—*PLEASE* MAN, I CAN'T— I CAN'T MOVE—FELICITY, HELP HIM!

An abrupt, terrified scream shatters the quiet evening.

DECLAN's eyes fixate on the gruesome spectacle unfolding before him, his body becoming rigid with shock.

DECLAN remains motionless, holding the keys in his hands.

FLICK remains asleep, eyes open.

The grisly sounds of the crocodile dragging its prey reverberate through the night.

DECLAN looks down at the keys still in his hand.

He looks back out beyond the gate.

Blackout.

END OF ACT ONE

ACT TWO

SCENE ONE

The sun beats down on the empty pool area. An eerie silence, punctuated with cicadas. The moment lingers.

The stillness is suddenly interrupted by JOHN, *as he enters from the motel gate, hauling a suitcase, clad in clothes inappropriate for the Darwin heat. He's sweating bullets as he juggles his belongings. He stares back at the mangroves he just ran through, catching his breath. He takes in the motel, a wild smile on his face.*

Suddenly, BOBBI *makes a dramatic entrance through the motel doorway, rushing towards* JOHN *as she carries the rat's cage.*

BOBBI: [*yelling*] Nuh uh, not today mister—

    JOHN *is screaming.*

JOHN: [*panicked*] I have a booking—I booked! I have a booking!
BOBBI: You what?
JOHN: I booked and everything!

    Beat.

BOBBI: Who are ya?
JOHN: I'm just John.
BOBBI: John?
JOHN: My name is Johnathan Quigley.
BOBBI: Quig?
JOHN: Quigley. Not Quig. I don't know a Quig.
BOBBI: Quigley.
JOHN: I had a booking. I saw you cancelled but I … like, I just thought … well I thought you might want to honour the reservation. I always honour the reservation. In America we, you know, we make promises and—I'm sorry …

    Beat. BOBBI *eyes him down, suspicious.*

BOBBI: We're closed. Everything's / closed.

JOHN: I know. I'm so sorry. I just, like, I had already arrived and—gosh, they put me in one of the airport lounges. But not a good lounge. It was awful. After a long flight? A tiny room, like a cage? I come from the United States of America. That's pretty far. And I didn't want to stay at the airport lounge. I like airports. I've only seen like two in my whole life. But I didn't come here to like, stay at the *airport*—I ran away, is what I'm saying. I ran away from the airport. Can you believe that? The lady was chasing me. She was actually bullying me.

Beat.

BOBBI: There are crocodiles.
JOHN: Yeah. I didn't know that, before I came. No-one told me. I'm just like, American.
BOBBI: You don't watch the news?
JOHN: It wasn't on the news. The news was busy.

Beat.

I have money. I even bought a travel money card.
BOBBI: That gate locked?
JOHN: I don't know—yeah, yeah. I just jumped over it.
BOBBI: Everyone's jumping over this gate.
JOHN: I do have money.
BOBBI: My name's Bobbi.
JOHN: That's an interesting name.

Beat.

And that's a good-looking rat.
BOBBI: Oh. You like her?
JOHN: This place is crazy.
BOBBI: Found her on the street. Lost little soul. Someone's gotta take care of / her.
JOHN: I'm sorry for barging in like this, I just ... I really wanted to stay in this motel. It's such a beautiful motel.
BOBBI: You joking?
JOHN: Nice pool and chairs.
BOBBI: Well I ... well look, we have a room. You're not allowed to go out though, are you, no you're not. And there's not too much to do here. Got a pool. A view, but ... some people get a bit weird

just hanging around all day. That's what my Mac said to me. My husband. He'd say, 'can't hang around all day'. He'd say that all the time. Not all the time, not every second! He's gotta sleep! Doesn't he? Yes he does. But, you can't just sit around. Life's short! Gotta dip your toes in the world sometimes, right?

JOHN: Right.

BOBBI: Right!

JOHN: Right as heck.

BOBBI: What?

JOHN: No, I agree, I'm saying I agree.

Beat.

BOBBI: We got a room. A room for Quiggles, hey? I'll get you some things. You look after Rosie for a sec?

JOHN: Yeah, no, of course. And thank you.

BOBBI: Don't you take your eyes off her, my precious little doll.

BOBBI *hands the cage over and begins to exit.*

JOHN: So are there uh, are there other people staying here?

BOBBI: [*offstage now*] Yeah yeah, a couple.

JOHN *peers into the cage. After a moment, he places it on the ground and inspects his surroundings, meandering towards the front of the stage.*

FLICK *enters from the motel doorway—unbeknownst to* JOHN—*dead in the eyes, sleepwalking. Slowly, she walks towards the cage,* JOHN *clocking her as he turns around.*

JOHN: Oh, hello there, my name is—

FLICK *picks the cage up and plunges it in the pool, holding it down.*

Oh heck! … Hey! Hey, hey—

He rushes and attempts to pry her hands off the cage. She's too strong.

Struggling, JOHN *eventually grabs the handle and places the cage beside the pool.*

FLICK *calmly resumes a spot on a deckchair, asleep.*

Uh. Um?

JOHN *splashes some water from the pool onto* FLICK*'s face. She wakes, furious.*

FLICK: Judas.

JOHN: You tried to drown the rat.

They stare at the cage.

FLICK: Fuck are you?

JOHN: Is it dead? It might be dead. Oh heck, please don't be dead.

FLICK: Where did you come from?

JOHN: [*picking up the cage.*] I don't know if it's wet and dead or just wet. I don't know what they're supposed to look like.

FLICK: Chill out—

JOHN: I've never had one. I've never had a pet. Bobbi, the lady, she—

FLICK: You know Bobbi?

JOHN: I just met Bobbi. Where is she? Said she would just / be a minute—

FLICK: How did you get here? We're not taking guests.

JOHN: I escaped from an airport lounge and I—*God* this is *crazy*! This is just a damn wild place isn't it? The heat and the crocodiles and the … *rat* drownings.

FLICK: You staying here?

JOHN: I have a booking. Bobbi said I could stay. So.

JOHN *dries the cage with his shirt and places it where it was. He stands for a moment, coming down off the adrenalin. He sits.*

Um. I think it's okay.

FLICK: You—

JOHN: I like your accent.

BOBBI *enters. Towels and a gown in hand.*

BOBBI: Ay. Flicky, this guy, Quiggles over here, blow me down, I thought it was a bloody break-in didn't I. Break-ins all the time here. Mac caught 'em one time. My husband, you should have seen him—beat the living shit out of 'em with a hatstand. He's liftin' this big old hatstand right above his head and just plowing it into them. Imagine that?

Pause.

Seen him?

ACT TWO

FLICK: Nuh.
BOBBI: Right. Never been away this long.
FLICK: He'll be back. Always comes back.
BOBBI: Thought he'd call or somethin'.
FLICK: You alright, Bob?
BOBBI: [*to* JOHN] I'll do a quick clean of your room and I'll come get ya. Flick, dunnies could do with a bit of a mop couldn't they? Yes they could.

    BOBBI *picks up the cage, peers in, weakly smiles and exits.*

JOHN: A dunny.
FLICK: It's a toilet.
JOHN: Guests have to clean their own toilets?
FLICK: What the—no, what? I work here.
JOHN: Oh.
FLICK: You know, there's an infestation.
JOHN: No-one told me about the infestation. I came here because—well, there are these devils everyone keeps talking about. Thought I'd see what all the fuss is. These devils sound crazy. With their feeding frenzies.
FLICK: They're Tasmanian Devils. They're in Tasmania. You came to the wrong part of the country.
JOHN: Oh. Sure?
FLICK: Yes.
JOHN: I don't know about that … but I actually came to find someone as well. A friend. I'm on a, like … soul-searching uh—
FLICK: Who?
JOHN: She's an author. Really great author. She's American too. Just need to ask her something.
FLICK: Renata Hartford?
JOHN: Oh. Yeah. Yeah! Is she here? Where is / she?
FLICK: She's my sister.
JOHN: No … I might just fricking faint. Gosh. Well. Hello. I am John Quigley.
FLICK: You a stalker? You stalk?
JOHN: No. Um. Maybe. No. I don't know. Not really. I mean we met at this thing, and uh, well our conversation got cut off and I just

needed to ask her something. I didn't know she had a ... I didn't know she had family here.
FLICK: You flew to the other side of the / world.
JOHN: It's hot here. Real hot.
FLICK: Think it will storm soon. You'll be fine.
JOHN: I don't think it's going to storm.
FLICK: I know when it's going to storm.
JOHN: Huh. Okay.
FLICK: What do you need to ask her?
JOHN: I'm doing the steps, in her book, and, well I'm just about done and I'm feeling a little um ... like I'm not finished. I still feel a bit uh, lost, yeah. But I'm close!
FLICK: That's super weird.
JOHN: I just really love that book.

Beat.

FLICK: You know, she's here with a guy? So I don't—
JOHN: Oh. Oh no no no I'm not like, trying to schtoop her.
FLICK: Schtoop?
JOHN: Is he Irish?
FLICK: Yeah, Irish.
JOHN: I saw him once.
FLICK: You what?
JOHN: Yeah I saw him. He can smell blood. Did you know that?

Beat.

FLICK: Everyone can smell blood.
JOHN: No but he's got like a crazy sensitivity to it. Renata told me.
FLICK: Hm.
JOHN: You don't think that's crazy?
FLICK: I don't know if that's true.
JOHN: Oh it's definitely true. Definitely. Renata is ... Did you like her book? That book is, you know, wow.
FLICK: Sure.
JOHN: It's ... the blood thing ... it's not like, a lie ... whatever, you had to be there.
FLICK: People lie.
JOHN: Not her.

ACT TWO 43

FLICK: That's a stupid thing to say.

Beat.

JOHN: Um. How long are they staying for?

FLICK: I don't know. He won't last much longer. He seems tense. Like he's about to snap.

JOHN: Because he can smell blood. Probably heaps of blood around here. I bet you he can smell blood really well. I could prove it probably.

FLICK: What's wrong with you?

JOHN: No, nothing. I just kind of feel like you're implying something here and I'm just, like, making it known that—you know. She's not a liar, so.

FLICK: Right. You prove it. You prove he can smell *blood.*

JOHN: Okay. Yeah.

FLICK: Hundred bucks.

JOHN: A hundred?

FLICK: A hundred if you prove—

A crash of thunder and lightning.

JOHN: Whoa. Oh. You were—

FLICK: I was right.

JOHN: I have goosebumps.

FLICK: You know, I've just like always been able to do that. Like I just know exactly when the storm's coming.

JOHN: That is so *fricking* cool.

FLICK: You think / so?

JOHN: What else can you do?

FLICK: Um. I don't know / actually.

JOHN: It *is* going to storm. You're incredible.

Beat. They watch as the clouds roll over.

FLICK: Well. Just so you're in the know. I'm having a party. You can come if you want. I don't care. But it's gonna be here. You're stuck anyway, so.

JOHN: The party is—what—out here?

FLICK: Yeah yeah. Well. Everywhere. Like this place is gonna be—like it's gonna be huge. Mega. Pumping. Fights and drug binges and cops. I dunno. You don't have to come, just like, if you / wanna.

JOHN: Is your sister going to come to / the party?
FLICK: I guess, yes.
JOHN: Where are you from?
FLICK: Here.
JOHN: But Renata's not—
FLICK: No. She's visiting me.
JOHN: Why is she American?
FLICK: My mum had sex all over the world.

Another crash of thunder.

Well. Prove the blood-sniffer. Hundred dollars.

BOBBI *enters from the motel doorway.*

BOBBI: Let's go Quiggles.

Fade to black.

SCENE TWO

Early morning. Dawn breaking over the swimming area. An eerie calm over the empty pool area.

DECLAN *emerges, looking worse for wear. He checks to see if he's alone and then cautiously makes his way towards the front of the pool area, almost unable to look directly out past the gate, afraid of what he might see. He pulls out a cigarette, lights it and begins to smoke.*

After a moment, JOHN, *wearing a motel gown, enters from the motel doorway. He catches a glimpse of* DECLAN's *back, hesitates, then retreats hastily into the doorway.*

A muffled cry from JOHN *is heard offstage.* DECLAN *momentarily lifts his head in the direction of the sound, then refocuses on his cigarette.*

JOHN *re-enters, holding one hand behind his back, faintly stained with blood.*

JOHN: Hello.

Beat.

Nice day.
DECLAN: Ah?
JOHN: Hot day.

ACT TWO

DECLAN: Yer, hot. Are you—sorry—
JOHN: How's / the—
DECLAN: Ah?
JOHN: How's the water?
DECLAN: Shite. Shite water.
JOHN: Do you smell something?
DECLAN: Water. Bit pissy. Pissy water.

Beat.

I didn't know there were—you just arrive or somethin'—have they opened up and all? People out and about?
JOHN: No, no. Just flew in. I didn't know about the like, the things.
DECLAN: They just let you / in?
JOHN: This is nice, Darwin. Very Aussie. Beautiful city you have here.
DECLAN: Not mine.
JOHN: Tell you, no-one back home knows about this place.
DECLAN: I could think of nicer / places.
JOHN: You see much wild life from here? Seen any crocodiles?

DECLAN looks at JOHN.

DECLAN: Maybe a bird. I've seen some birds. Annoyin'.
JOHN: You heard of these devils? They got these giant mouse things in Australia. Tasmanian Devils. I thought they were here but apparently they're not in Darwin. Damn. Was hoping to see one. Was hoping to see them like, tear some rats to shreds, you know?

Beat.

DECLAN: Good luck to yer, man.

DECLAN rises to exit.

JOHN: I think I saw someone die.
DECLAN: What did yer say?
JOHN: I came here—arrived yesterday. I was waiting at the carousel and one by one I saw everyone take their bags. You know how people get after flights. Just courtesy out the window, really. They're all ravaging through these bags like animals. I had a guy—there was a guy like that. Annoying looking kinda guy, like, quite muscular and just like, had an attitude? I hate attitudes. And he saw his bag. And he just fricken pummelled his way through, and he tries to lift

his bag up off the carousel? But it's stuck? There's like a strap stuck in a bit of the carousel? And he's pulling and he's pulling but it just isn't coming out. So he jumps on the carousel!? Like a maniac. And he's heaving and swearing. And we can all see that the bag is about to go through the thing—the tunnel—but he doesn't see that. And so he gives another pull on his bag, and he slips and smacks his head like a baseball bat against the top of the tunnel thing. Huge gash on his forehead. Blood pouring out like his head was urinating. He got blood all over everyone's bags. And then I think he might've died. I'd be shocked if he didn't die.

Beat.

DECLAN: I'm sorry that happened to yer. That's an awful thing.
JOHN: Yeah! Just like a river of blood. At the thing. At the airport.
DECLAN: Christ.
JOHN: It smelled real bad.
DECLAN: Have we met or somethin'?
JOHN: Have we?

Beat.

They stare at each other.

DECLAN: Why're you lookin at me like that?
JOHN: What?
DECLAN: You're lookin' at me all weird. What you lookin' at?
JOHN: Your accent is really difficult to understand. I don't know how anyone could really understand / you.
DECLAN: Fuck yer talkin' / about?
JOHN: I'm just trying to understand if you understand what I'm saying.
DECLAN: What *are* you saying?
JOHN: What I just said.
DECLAN: About the man at the airport?
JOHN: Yes, the man at the airport. It's what I said. Isn't it?

Beat.

DECLAN: You are a strange little man.

A baby's cries are heard.

JOHN: That sounds like a baby.

DECLAN: It's a baby.
JOHN: Oh. So … whose—

> DECLAN *turns towards the sound.*
>
> *He exits, passing* BOBBI *on his way out, who strolls past with her rat.*
>
> *There's something off—she's not as chirpy as usual.*

Ouch. Ouch ouch ouch.

> JOHN *looks at his hand.*

Please help me. I cut my—I can't believe I—I'm squeamish. Do you have a bandage or something? Do I need a shot? Like a tetanus shot?

> BOBBI *looks at* JOHN, *looks at his hand.*

BOBBI: Give me a sec, take her.

> BOBBI *turns to exit, leaving the cage with* JOHN.
>
> *The baby cries.*

JOHN: Whose baby is that?
BOBBI: Your new friends', Quiggles.

> BOBBI *exits.*
>
> JOHN *wonders, then flinches in pain. He can't look at his bloody hand, the confident exterior in the face of* DECLAN *eradicated.*
>
> RENATA *enters, freezing upon seeing* JOHN. *He's frozen too.*
>
> *Pause.*

RENATA: Uh.
JOHN: Yeah. Um.
RENATA: I didn't know anyone else was here.
JOHN: Oh. John?
RENATA: No.
JOHN: No?
RENATA: No, I'm not John.
JOHN: No, I'm John. Quigley.
RENATA: Oh. Have they opened up the—
JOHN: We like, met. Like … we met … last week.
RENATA: I wasn't here last week. Is that blood?

JOHN: No in New York … at the party. With the oyster fork. You said maybe I should come to—do you not remember me?

   Beat.

RENATA: Why are you here?

JOHN: Well just … like your book, you know. Follow your gut kinda thing and I wanted—I'm not here to like *schtoop* you if that's what you're—

RENATA: *Schtoop* me?

JOHN: You told me it would be a good idea to come here maybe. So … feeling a bit damn silly, but um, well I thought this would be good for me, to come here, to find you and I don't know. Took your words to heart. But … well I just wanted to see the world through your eyes, honestly. Maybe learn from you or … Hey, um, weird question, do you have a baby?

   Beat.

RENATA: I am glad you liked my book.

JOHN: It's really very good.

RENATA: We should talk later. If you don't have plans. You don't have plans here, do you?

JOHN: No. Not really. We can talk! Is that like an a.m. or p.m. kind of thing?

RENATA: p.m.

JOHN: Like tonight.

RENATA: Yes.

   Beat.

Someone needs to let that rat go.

   RENATA *exits.*

   JOHN *looks at the rat. Slowly, he walks towards it.*

   BOBBI *enters, startling* JOHN.

   She approaches him and begins to wrap a bandage around his hand.

BOBBI: In the wars, are we?

JOHN: Oh yeah. I'm just like, yeah, I'm a pretty wild guy. Always getting into crazy situations.

BOBBI: I'm sure you are, Quiggles.

ACT TWO

JOHN: You ever think about letting that rat go?
BOBBI: Ah?
JOHN: The rat? Maybe it needs to run around. You know. If it's a wild rat.
BOBBI: Seems alright. Wish people would mind their business.
JOHN: Oh, no, I was just making conversation.
BOBBI: Just a pet, Quigley.
JOHN: No, I know. Pets are good. My dad just bought like a rescue dog, and like, my mum died so it's been real good for him. He like watches CNN with the dog and talks to her about what he thinks. I think sometimes he pretends the dog's my mum. Like he'll say, 'I know I know Maggie, I shouldn't get worked up, you're right'. Like to the dog. It's yeah. It's cute.

Silence.

A long moment in which BOBBI *straps* JOHN*'s hand.*

BOBBI: Your dad's alone?
JOHN: Um. Well yeah. He's got the dog, so. But yeah. He's alone.

Pause.

BOBBI *slowly but surely, begins to cry.*

JOHN: Oh heck. I'm sorry. I hope I didn't, like, I was just saying—
BOBBI: [*whispering*] I don't know where my husband is.
JOHN: Oh.
BOBBI: I think he may have left.
JOHN: Oh. He just left?
BOBBI: Yeah left. Somethin' better out there for him maybe.
JOHN: Oh. Well, hey, you know. There's really no point lingering on the past. Yeah. I've learnt that. No point in crying when you think about it. Humans are weird like that, with crying. There's no point. Just gotta keep going.
BOBBI: No point in crying?
JOHN: I don't think so.
BOBBI: How can you ... I feel it in my bones. A sadness. I'm sad without him. Don't like being sad.
JOHN: I guess ... yeah. I just ... sometimes you must put yourself first. It's good to be independent—you should really read this book, Renata, in there, she—

BOBBI: You only have so long. Don't you. And he knows me. I like him watching me. I like him knowin' me. I like sharin' with him. Memories and that, you know? I told him, I said Mac we've still got all these things we're going to do together. We still got excitement, we still got dreams and … I didn't want him to get bored of me. But I think he did.

> JOHN *pauses, then slowly nods.*

Fade to black.

SCENE THREE

Afternoon. The pool area of The Palms Motel. A large tourist map of Darwin is strewn out in front of a sweaty, manic, crouching RENATA. *She holds a pen, making careful notations, a notepad beside her.*

DECLAN, *looking even more dishevelled, watches her intently from his deckchair.*

The baby cot sits beside him.

A long pause before dialogue.

DECLAN: Ren.

RENATA: Hm?

DECLAN: I'd like to say something. Got an / announcement.

RENATA: Amazing.

DECLAN: I would like you to promise me something.

RENATA: Can you read a map?

DECLAN: I want you to promise me that we're leaving on Sunday.

RENATA: Might not be able to. They haven't said anything.

DECLAN: Should be prepared in any case.

RENATA: It's Felicity's birthday tomorrow. I said I'd help her organise the party.

DECLAN: What party?

RENATA: Motel party.

DECLAN: Well, that's … okay, so you do that and then we leave on / Sunday.

RENATA: See this here? That's Fogg Dam Conservation Reserve. It has pythons.

DECLAN: Ren.

ACT TWO

RENATA: And Crocosaurus Cove.
DECLAN: Ah?
RENATA: That's where you swim with the crocodiles. They call it the cage of death.
DECLAN: What're you doin' with this?
RENATA: Yeah.
DECLAN: Ren.
RENATA: What?

Beat.

DECLAN: Not good for Lily out here.
RENATA: She's got no idea what's going on. I'm allowed to live a little / still.
DECLAN: We're going home for good. That's my announcement. You, Lily and I. She needs a home. Permanently. I'm insisting. You could write the book there. Could write about Galway.
RENATA: Write what about Galway?
DECLAN: Good content in Galway. You'll get to meet Rob.
RENATA: Paedophile Rob?
DECLAN: No, that's other Rob. That's a different Rob. You won't meet him.
RENATA: Could you look at this and—
DECLAN: Hey. I'm serious.

RENATA *stops and looks at him.*

RENATA: You think we're going to live a nice little life in Galway do you?
DECLAN: We've made these plans for months. Have to follow through. So you'll live with it. Not debating it with yer.
RENATA: All sounds very fucking / familiar.
DECLAN: Ma and Da are ready for us, Lily's dying from the heat out here, I need to be back home before I have a fucken breakdown— just need you to let go of whatever yer doin' here and then we can leave. There's not even a funeral.
RENATA: I don't think she's dead.
DECLAN: Excuse me?
RENATA: I think Flick lied to me. I think she's just gone. Gone out running. That's why there's no funeral.
DECLAN: Well, isn't that kind of an important thing to ask 'er?
RENATA: It doesn't matter.

DECLAN: Then what in the hell are we doing here?
RENATA: It's her birthday. I think she wanted me here for her birthday. She doesn't have any friends. She doesn't have anything.
DECLAN: We're here for a pity party, are we? For your fucken loner sister? We're going home, Ren. Everyone's in agreement apart from you.
RENATA: What? So your parents, Lily, you, you've gotten together and had a brainstorm about this have you? Made a little choice for me.
DECLAN: You're her mother.
RENATA: Said you wouldn't do this again. Do you remember that?

Beat.

DECLAN: Do what … This is different.
RENATA: Different, sure.
DECLAN: We both had the baby Ren. Together. Half my brain, half your brain.
RENATA: No.
DECLAN: What 'no'?
RENATA: No. That's wrong.

Pause.

DECLAN: Doesn't matter. Bobbi's given me a number for a car to the airport and all. Just don't want to be late on Sunday. Want to get one of them neck pillows too. And a coffee. Proper coffee.
RENATA: [*under her breath*] You cornered me into motherhood Declan.
DECLAN: Yer what?
RENATA: You heard me.
DECLAN: It's not a fucken death sentence. You had a baby. It's done. Get over it. Move / on.
RENATA: I had to have it. Didn't have to keep it.
DECLAN: What do you want me to tell you? We have 'er. And I love 'er. And you love 'er. Can't just throw her over the fence.
RENATA: Could have given her up. Given her to someone who wants her.
DECLAN: I want her.
RENATA: Help me with this map Declan.
DECLAN: I want our baby, Renata.
RENATA: No. You want this little … this little made-up life you have in your head.

ACT TWO

DECLAN: Not talkin' 'bout this again. That's / it.
RENATA: You didn't talk to me about it in the first place. Remember? I'm enforcing. I'm insisting. 'No baby of mine' ... And that was it. You cornered me. Five months pregnant with no idea and then yep, okay, this is us now. And you thought you'd get away with the well-trodden roadmap of a mother I'm meant to follow, huh? And you can play the excited father. Because you have *nothing* else going on.

Beat.

I'm not following that roadmap.
DECLAN: Can't just be givin' a baby away to any ol' fella.
RENATA: Any old what? What does that even mean? It's *adoption*.
DECLAN: We did the right thing. *Did somethin'*. Sometimes you got to do something, make things right. Action things. Take some responsibility.
RENATA: No. That was inaction. She's just here now. She's just ... around. For something to talk about. For something to reference. So you can say you *have* one, instead of—
DECLAN: You think I had a baby so I could have / something to *do*?
RENATA: —instead of having her somewhere better. Because you wouldn't do / something about it.
DECLAN: You think that fucken little of me / do yer?
RENATA: Because you were scared of what Ma and Da would say. Because / you thought I would come around, didn't you?
DECLAN: You're her mother. Out of the question, adoption. Cold-blooded is what it is. Wasn't goin' to let that happen. Because you're not. You're not cold-blooded.
RENATA: Don't tell me what I am.

Pause.

DECLAN: I need you to try and meet me in the world I live in because that's the world I want Lil to grow up in. The real world. No stories, no drama, no make-believe.
RENATA: You're asking me to pretend.
DECLAN: No. You're pretending now.

Beat.

I do love yer. Just ... yeah. I feel that. I love / yer.

RENATA: [*whispering*] No you don't. You don't feel things. You just want things.

Pause.

DECLAN: Ren. I saw something horrible the other night. Felicity and I … I was out here, just havin' some air, and well … and I think I saw something horrible, and we didn't do anything, and I can't … has she said anything to yer? Did Felicity talk to yer?

BOBBI *enters with a cleaning trolley.* DECLAN *sits upright, alert.*

Bobbi.

BOBBI: Hello.

DECLAN: Hi. Hello. Um. Any news?

BOBBI: Sunday they think we can leave. Christmas Eve. Just announced. One more day of this.

DECLAN: Okay. Okay great, that's just—perfect. I'll—I'll call Da—organise the pick-up and—we can still be back in time for Christmas / I think, yer—

BOBBI: You / leavin'?

RENATA: We might be hungover from the party.

BOBBI: You havin' a party?

RENATA: Flick's having a / party.

DECLAN: One more day.

BOBBI: Last time her mum had a party round here it was chaos wasn't it, yes it was, bloody / chaos.

RENATA: Well Felicity's not her mother.

BOBBI: Mac used to love those parties. He did, yes, oh he did like them.

Beat. BOBBI *walks towards the gate.*

DECLAN: [*yelling*] STOP!

BOBBI: What?

RENATA: Declan.

DECLAN: What?

BOBBI: What's wrong? Just checkin' that gate's closed.

DECLAN: Fine. Sorry. I'm fine.

Beat.

BOBBI: Seen our guest? Nice fellow. Bit strange, but a nice fellow. Wide-eyed little American.

DECLAN: Yer. I met 'im.
RENATA: Did you?
DECLAN: American guy. Kind of … kind of just a fucked-up guy.
BOBBI: I'll check in with youse later. Lost my keys again.
DECLAN: Oh, Bobbi, I—I got yer keys. Yer, do you—yer keys.

> DECLAN *hands over the keys.*
>
> BOBBI *looks at him.*

BOBBI: Why'd you have my keys?
DECLAN: Found 'em the other night, I … You shouldn't just leave 'em lyin' around. Keys are … important. Important, those are.

> *Beat.*

BOBBI: Okay.

> BOBBI *exits.*

RENATA: There are these devils here. Do you know this? Giant rats with crazy teeth. And they get all psychotic? When they feed?

> *Beat.*

DECLAN: Who told you that?
RENATA: What?
DECLAN: Who told you that?
RENATA: I don't know.

> *Fade to black.*

SCENE FOUR

Same day, early evening. Dusk settles. The illuminated pool casts an eerie glow over the motel's deserted courtyard. RENATA, *feeling the heat but with a strange calmness, sits, cross-legged on a deckchair.*

JOHN *enters quietly.* RENATA *turns to face him. A moment of tension.*

JOHN: Hi.
RENATA: Hello.
JOHN: Hi.
RENATA: Yeah. So you just came here.
JOHN: Well … you told me to come here.
RENATA: When?

JOHN: At the party thing. Didn't you? And your book says, you know. Your book says like, lean into the … never mind.

> *Beat.*

RENATA: How did you find / me?

JOHN: Micah told me. Yeah. From the party. Did you know he has to wear an eyepatch for a bit now? Because of the fork? He told me one of his eyes looks like a vagina.

> *Beat.*

Just in case you were wondering how he was.

RENATA: What do you want to happen now?

> *Beat.* JOHN *thinks.*

JOHN: Um. Honestly, I just feel like uh I've kind of given up a lot of my life because of that book and well now I feel a bit … well I didn't know you had a baby. Because your book says like, don't do that. I wasn't expecting … But if you could just tell me what I should do next? I did come all this way.

> *Beat.* RENATA *thinks.*

RENATA: I have been writing. There's lots to write about here.

JOHN: So much.

RENATA: You want to know something? I've been sneaking out. I've been running through the mangroves.

JOHN: Oh my god, samesies.

RENATA: Yeah?

JOHN: Well. Once. I ran through the mangroves once. When I was escaping the airport hotel.

RENATA: Feels good, doesn't it?

JOHN: I mean yeah. Not really. I don't know. This is cool though. This motel—

RENATA: Do you want to know a secret?

JOHN: Yes. Please.

RENATA: I'm leaving. Tomorrow.

JOHN: Back to New York?

RENATA: No. Just out there.

JOHN: Right. Out there?

ACT TWO

RENATA: I'm going to start back at the mangroves, East Point Reserve, with the mud up to my knees. That's where the real crocodiles are. Not Crocosaurus Cove. Not a petting zoo. I want to see the real ones. And then it's bushland, a long walk but then you hit a national park with termite mounds and waterfalls—I'll climb a waterfall probably. And then it's Mary River, more crocodiles, bigger ones apparently. You can see their eyes in the night. You have to swim to get across the river. But that's the thrill. And then eventually, I don't know how long, eventually there's Kakadu. Ubirr Rock. Gunlom Falls. People have died there. I'm just going to go. Leap into it. So.

Beat.

Do you want to come with me?
JOHN: You want me to come with you?
RENATA: Why not?
JOHN: Oh, yes. Yeah. Cool, like but … hm … I guess like, what would you need me to do? Like an assistant? Or like a butler or something—
RENATA: Like a leap of faith. Like a shot in the dark.

Beat.

You left your home, your job, your dying mother—
JOHN: My father.
RENATA: That's right. I remember. Adventure, huh? This is going to be the wildest story of my life yet. You must be there for it. You know, the book doesn't really mean anything if you don't follow through. You can do all the steps, and it's good you did, but you still have to … take risks, I suppose.

Beat.

JOHN: I met your sister. Flick. I like her.
RENATA: What?
JOHN: Your sister. She's real interesting.
RENATA: She's fine.
JOHN: Don't you need to, like, look after your baby and Declan and all—
RENATA: No.
JOHN: You can just *tell* me what's in the new / book.

RENATA: This. This is the next step. You come with me. What else did you come here for?
JOHN: Yeah.

Pause.

You know uh, you know how you told me about the devils?
RENATA: You told me about the devils.
JOHN: No but you said you'd seen them.
RENATA: Yeah, we can go and see the devils.
JOHN: But they're not here. They're in Tasmania. They don't even live here.
RENATA: They do though.
JOHN: But they don't. I like, checked.

Beat.

Does Declan know you're leaving?
RENATA: He doesn't.
JOHN: Won't that upset him?
RENATA: He'll be fine. He's got a good sense for things. You know he can—
JOHN: Yeah the blood. He can smell blood. Right?

Beat. RENATA *stares.*

RENATA: He'll be fine on his own. He'll be a great father.
JOHN: But how could you leave your baby?
RENATA: Why? Because I'm her mother?

A crash of thunder, lightning.

The pair look up at the sky above them.

JOHN: I think I owe—I just remembered—
RENATA: I'm leaving tomorrow. Eight o'clock. A.m. Think about it.
JOHN: It's your sister's birthday tomorrow.

Fade to black.

SCENE FIVE

Late evening. FLICK *is nestled in a deckchair, staring at the rippling water.*

JOHN *sits next to her, the pair drinking bottles of beer. They're playing a game of Two Truths and a Lie.*

FLICK: I am a certified deep-water diver.
JOHN: Okay. Okay, hm.
FLICK: Okay?
JOHN: Yeah.
FLICK: I sleep with my eyes open.
JOHN: How does that work?
FLICK: I have like a condition. I think. I sleep a lot, right? Like I just fall asleep very quickly when—
JOHN: Like narcolepsy?
FLICK: Maybe. Maybe. I don't know. It happens when I feel … it just happens sometimes. But my eyes stay open. Like I'm seeing things but I'm not seeing things.
JOHN: Hm. Okay. Sure …
FLICK: Okay next / one?
JOHN: How would you know if your eyes are open? If you're, like, sleeping?
FLICK: My mum used to tell me.
JOHN: Oh.
FLICK: Yeah.
JOHN: Okay.
FLICK: Okay, last one. I have never left Darwin in my whole life, and I never will.

    Beat.

JOHN: There's no way you're a deep-water diver.
FLICK: Oh my God? Oh my God! Correct. That was really good. How did you—
JOHN: I feel like if you've never left Darwin you're kind of unlikely to be a deep-diver. Like if you're not, you know, into adventure or whatever. Not that you're not, but, you know what I mean.

FLICK: Yeah. I know what you mean.
JOHN: And I don't think you would like, bring up that sleep thing—with your mum—like, if that wasn't true. Considering, she's like … yeah.

Beat.

FLICK: Okay. Your turn.
JOHN: Okay two truths and a …

Beat.

I'm worried my dad might die kind of soon.

Beat.

FLICK: True.
JOHN: Yeah.
FLICK: What's he got?
JOHN: Alzheimer's.
FLICK: Shit, man.
JOHN: Yeah. He's a weird guy.

Pause.

I think I maybe shouldn't have jumped off the deep end like this. To come here. Pretty insane of me.
FLICK: Hm. Maybe.

Beat.

You know, you're on the other side of the world. You ran away from the airport. You got chased and you survived! You saved a rat. You've had an adventure. I've never travelled. So, you're doing something. You should be proud.
JOHN: Yeah.
FLICK: Yeah.
JOHN: Just kind of feel like maybe I'm letting him down. Even though he doesn't—he doesn't really know what's going on. But. He's sick. And it's scary. And I ran away.

Beat.

FLICK: My mum was unwell. She was really unwell. And like, lost. And it's funny, you know, she had my sister in America and had a bit of a freak out I guess. Just left her so she didn't have to deal with it. I don't know why she came here. To Darwin. Good place for drifters maybe. But she had me here when she didn't really know who she was. So, she couldn't really be my mum until she sorted that out. And then she kind of kept running away. Over and over again. People do that, you know. It's normal, I think. The world's scary. It's scary right now.

Beat.

I just like, waited for her. Like I didn't go to school, and I didn't make any friends and I didn't … do anything. Because in my mind it was temporary. I thought she'd find whatever she was looking for. And I waited for her. Because she's my mum. She was my mum. But I don't want to wait around anymore.

Silence.

JOHN: You should travel.
FLICK: I should.
JOHN: We could go travelling.
FLICK: Hah. Yeah. Maybe.

DECLAN *enters, drunk, beer in hand.*

DECLAN: Alright.

He stumbles over to sit with them.

Hope I'm not interrupting.
FLICK: You stink.
DECLAN: That's rich.
JOHN: I might head / off.
DECLAN: Tom.
JOHN: John.
DECLAN: What you both doing out here?
FLICK: Talking.

DECLAN *looks at* JOHN, *suspicious.*

Where's Ren?
DECLAN: What're you doin' here, Jim?
FLICK: Go to bed Declan.

DECLAN *sits.*

DECLAN: You got any drink?
JOHN: I have more / beer.

FLICK: He doesn't need anything / dude.
DECLAN: Yer / I do.
JOHN: I'll get you some. I guess? I don't—yeah I'll get you some. Maybe I'll / have another.
FLICK: He's going to piss / himself.
DECLAN: Thank you, Mr Ripley.

> JOHN *exits.*

Why you hangin' round him?
FLICK: He's funny.
DECLAN: You should meet some new people, Felicity. Don't know how you do it. Sittin' round here all day. Waitin' for somethin' to happen. What a hellhole this is. This in-between shithole. Transient, bullshit. Just a pool and a fucken American.
FLICK: You should leave then.
DECLAN: I am. First thing Sunday. She's comin' with me. Sail this ship right—

> JOHN *re-enters, beers in hand.*

Ah, Timothy with the goods.
JOHN: John.
DECLAN: What brings you all the way from—where you from? What do yer do?
JOHN: Um. I'm from Pennsylvania. I was at an insurance company.
DECLAN: Bored, were yer?
JOHN: Yeah, I guess yeah.
DECLAN: Wanted some excitement did yer? Thought there was more to life ah?
JOHN: Yeah I guess so.
DECLAN: You found it? You feel like a good little spiritual traveller now ah? You found those devils you lookin' for?
FLICK: Declan shut / up.

> DECLAN *sneezes suddenly, then inhales deeply through his nose.*

JOHN: Can I ask you a question?
DECLAN: Got a little question does he?
JOHN: Can you smell blood?

> *Beat.*

ACT TWO 63

DECLAN: What?
JOHN: I'm just wondering. Can you smell it?
DECLAN: What does that even mean, smell blood? What does it smell like?
JOHN: Don't know.

DECLAN eyes FLICK.

DECLAN: You told him did yer?
FLICK: Told him what?
DECLAN: What do you know, huh, Tim?
JOHN: I don't know—
FLICK: Have you lost the / fucken plot.
DECLAN: What'd you tell him? That it was my fault? That's why he keeps lookin' at me. Like I'm / an animal.
FLICK: What the fuck are you talking about? We weren't even talking about you.
DECLAN: Not just my fault. Don't know why *you* didn't do nothin'. Watchin' a man torn to shreds, gobbled up like that. You saw it too, not just me, can't blame it all on me. Why does everyone blame everythin' on me? It's on *both* of us to—like I'm responsible for everyone am I? Everyone's too fucken crazy to take some of the reins, are they?

DECLAN*'s on the verge of a breakdown.*

JOHN: What did you do?
DECLAN: Nothing. I couldn't do anything. I just watched him. The poor man.
JOHN: What poor man?
FLICK: Declan, what are you—
DECLAN: A man, I don't know I … there was a man … you saw him, he … you know he …

DECLAN *begins to slur wildly.*

I couldn't help him. I couldn't move, I was just a tiny boy, twelve I was, yer. They were puttin' in all this security at me school. They were puttin' up this like structure, like this large metallic fence kind of thing. Big construction and that. Richie, my best mate, great lad, Richie, we thought we'd just … wreck it. So we meet up, middle of the night, you know, feelin' all excited and that. Stupid. We make it to the school and there's like a crane yer? We thought we'd climb the crane. So, Richie hops up first and he only got a wee bit up there and he slipped. And there's this er, jagged metal thing, pokin' out just under him. Falls right on it. Starts bleedin' out. Blood fucken everywhere, like a pool, and I … I didn't do anythin'. Like I couldn't move? I couldn't … I literally couldn't … move. And he just died. I felt so uh … Terrible feelin' that. To not be in control when someone's hurtin'.

Beat.

To freeze. You know, Flick? Like the other night. With the poor man at the gate. He didn't see the croc comin' up. You saw 'im. We was there. Why didn't we open the gate … You froze too.

Beat.

FLICK: Declan. I think I was sleeping.

DECLAN *begins to cry.*

DECLAN: He was whistling. The man was whistling.

Fade to black.

SCENE SIX

The next morning, dawn. Flick's birthday.
JOHN *and* FLICK *are asleep, sharing a deckchair.*
RENATA *sits on an opposing deckchair, watching them, curious.*
Eventually JOHN *wakes, frozen at the sight of* RENATA.

JOHN: Oh. Hi.
RENATA: Hello.
JOHN: Hey.
RENATA: So.
JOHN: I should—I might go have a shower. Kind of stink.
RENATA: Right.

Beat.

JOHN: I don't know if … I think you should maybe wait. If you're still thinking of leaving. It's her birthday. And the party.

ACT TWO

RENATA: Yes.

> JOHN *exits.*
>
> RENATA *sits for a bit, watching* FLICK.
>
> *Eventually* BOBBI *enters, holding her rat in its cage.*
>
> *She holds a finger to her lips and beams at* RENATA, *who weakly nods.*
>
> BOBBI *suddenly begins to sing happy birthday at the top of her voice, waking* FLICK.

FLICK: Jesus—
BOBBI: Happy birthday Flicky.
FLICK: Thank you Bob.
RENATA: Happy—
BOBBI: One more day locked in! One more isn't it, yes, it is, one more.
FLICK: Yeah. Yeah weird. Do we have bookings?
BOBBI: Few. Gonna be busy soon I reckon. Lots of them backpackers passing through finally. With their drinking. Ha ha! They do drink. Looking for love. For romance. The spontaneity.
FLICK: People do drink.
BOBBI: Got ya a pressie.

> BOBBI *retrieves an envelope from her pocket, opens it up and reads a letter aloud.*

Dear Miss Flick. While it's a crying shame to spend your birthday locked inside The Palms Motel, in a way, it all makes sense. It's our home, our little sanctuary here away from the mess of the world, a corner of chaos, I like to call it. I want to thank you. For everything. For being the glue that holds my little life together. For being like a daughter to me. Don't know what I'd do without … So, it might not sound like much, but I have here a Promise Voucher for you. No questions, no eye-rolling, just one wish granted, whatever it may be. Whenever it may be. Hand it over when you're ready, and your favour shall be granted, missy. Happy birthday, and all the mushy stuff that comes with it. I love you.

> FLICK *rises and hugs* BOBBI.
>
> *A baby crying.*

RENATA *exits as they hug.*

FLICK: Fucken really sweet, / thanks.

BOBBI: Clean your mouth out Flick.

Beat.

FLICK: Bobbi I think I need to tell you / something.

BOBBI: I got some tequila. Mac, he used to love parties. Oh yeah, we'd both be up and about, dancing, kissing, gettin' crazy. Didn't we, yes we did. Been a long time since we done that.

There's a sudden sadness between the both of them.

FLICK: Bobbi. Declan ...

BOBBI: Ah?

FLICK: Um. Declan said ... I don't know what happened exactly, but Declan kinda said that, yeah, he saw a man, out there. The other night. I think maybe he was trying to open the gate.

BOBBI: Right.

FLICK: And I don't know but ... he said he was whistling.

Beat.

BOBBI: Mac? My Mac?! I knew he'd come / back—

FLICK: It was the other night—

BOBBI: Maaac! Maaaaaac! Where is he?

Beat.

Flick? Where's Mac?

FLICK: I'm so sorry Bobbi.

BOBBI: About what?

FLICK: I think Declan saw Mac get taken by one.

Silence.

I don't know what really happened. But he saw a man, he was whistling, he came to the gate? I think? And Declan just didn't get the gate open in time. And yeah. There was a croc and ...

Beat.

BOBBI *screams.*

FLICK *jolts up to comfort her.*

Bobbi, Bobbi—

BOBBI: What do you mean 'in time'? What the fuck was he doing?
FLICK: Think he kind of panicked. I don't think he knew what to do.
BOBBI: What to do?! You see a man being attacked, you scream, you fight, you call the cops, you *tell* me, you do SOMETHING! That was my *fucking* husband, Flick!

Pause.

FLICK: I know.

Beat.

BOBBI *slouches. Crying. Defeated.*

BOBBI: The man did nothing. But he knew what he was doin'.
FLICK: I don't really know what happened.
BOBBI: Maybe better not really knowing.
FLICK: You know, Mum's gone and, if it was Mac, well … maybe they're both out there somewhere. Together.
BOBBI: Your mother's missing. My husband is dead.

Beat.

Might need a moment Flicky.
FLICK: No, yeah. I should …

FLICK *gets up to leave.*

We don't have to have this party.

FLICK *turns to go and is almost inside when* BOBBI *calls out.*

BOBBI: We're havin' the party. It's important. Go tell Quiggles.
FLICK: Okay.

FLICK *slowly exits.* BOBBI *takes a moment, peering into the rat's cage.*

BOBBI: Time to go, huh, missy?

BOBBI *approaches the front of the stage and exits towards the motel gate.*

An eerie silence over the motel pool area until eventually, RENATA *enters.*

She starts to hang decorations for the party.

Fade to black.

SCENE SEVEN

Same day, evening.

An air of anticipation.

FLICK *and* JOHN *put the finishing touches on the pool area.*

JOHN: At my old work, at this company, they used to like delegate organising the cakes and whatever to different people. And I swear there was like a birthday every week—like it was all the time. And every time they'd hand out the delegations I'd be like please no, no, no, no, no don't give it to me. Because it's awkward. What if I get the wrong cake or whatever. Anyway so I got it this one time, last year, for this woman, Shyani, and she had all these allergies so I had to drive to this specific place and get it and it was this whole thing. So I get there, and it's like really snowing like crazy, and I've got fifty dollars in cash to spend from the company. I've got it in my hand. But I lost the fifty dollars in the snow? Because, like, I'm so stupid and I was like whatever, it's fifty dollars. And I go in and I went to pay with my credit card, and I noticed that she'd made a mistake, the woman at the counter, she added an extra zero so it was five hundred dollars?

FLICK: Right.

JOHN: But I just … like I just paid it. Like I didn't say anything.

FLICK: What—Why did you do that?

JOHN: I don't even know, like I was scared?

FLICK: That's five hundred dollars dude.

JOHN: Isn't that crazy?

FLICK: That's psychotic.

JOHN: I know but I've always had this thing, like, so what? It's five hundred dollars. It's a cake. There are like people dying every day everywhere and I'm just like in my dad's apartment. And I didn't want to embarrass the woman at the counter. Isn't that stupid?

FLICK: Did Shyani like the cake?

JOHN: I don't know. Shyani didn't really talk to me ever.

FLICK: I'm sorry.

JOHN: It's so fine.

ACT TWO

FLICK: You know I've never seen snow.
JOHN: It doesn't snow here?
FLICK: Uh. No. Sometimes I think I'm so used to the heat that if I saw snow I might just turn into an icecube right away.
JOHN: It's snowing right now at home.
FLICK: Wow.
JOHN: What?
FLICK: I'd just like, that'd be sick. If I could see that.
JOHN: Oh. I could show you. If you / wanted—
FLICK: You speak to your dad?
JOHN: Yeah. I called him.
FLICK: I'd love to see snow.

BOBBI enters, dressed up, looking flash.

BOBBI: Ay.
FLICK: Did you set this all up?
BOBBI: Ah?
FLICK: Where'd you get all this from?
BOBBI: Thought it was you, darls.
JOHN: You look fricken great Bobbi.
BOBBI: Oh please, well yes, well, I do know how to dress up don't I, yes I do. Nice to dress up sometimes I think, yes it is. Have to sometimes. Smile on, dress on, drinks in. Hah. Um. Yeah.
FLICK: You look amazing. Where's Rosie?
BOBBI: Oh, you know, yeah just—though it was time, didn't I. Let her go. Time for her to do her thing really. Don't think she was liking that cage much. Hope she's alright out there.
JOHN: She'll be great out there.
FLICK: You didn't set this up? You seen / Renata?
BOBBI: No, no. Looks amazing darls. Still a few things to hang up though hey? A party. I do love a party.

DECLAN enters.

DECLAN: Alright.
FLICK: You guys gonna come join?
DECLAN: Yer. Just packin' up and that.
FLICK: Could have a drink though?
DECLAN: Yer. No. And happy returns and all that, you know.

FLICK: Thank you.
BOBBI: Flick, you wanna grab us some tequila ay? It's in the very backroom, bring it all out, there's some champers and all kinds of things in there. You two go fetch it ah? Irish can finish these beautiful decorations with me. Can't you, Irish?
DECLAN: Well I—
BOBBI: You got time, Irish.

>   *Beat.*

FLICK: No worries Bob.

>   JOHN *and* FLICK *exit.*

>   DECLAN *looks at* BOBBI, *perhaps a little nervous.*

DECLAN: Nice dress there.
BOBBI: Thank you.
DECLAN: Er. What you want me to do?
BOBBI: Hang them up. Make 'em look pretty.
DECLAN: Got a few things to do—
BOBBI: Havin' a drink though, aren't ya?
DECLAN: Yer. Sure.

>   DECLAN *begins to hang decorations up, his back to* BOBBI.

You know, er, thanks for havin' us and all. Sorry if we were a bit all over the place. Just a weird time. Weird time in the world at the moment isn't it? Chaotic. Everyone's panicking.

>   RENATA *enters, backpack swung on her shoulder.*

>   *She freezes as she clocks both* BOBBI *and* DECLAN.

>   *A tense stand-off between* BOBBI *and* RENATA.

>   *Eventually,* BOBBI *clocks what's happening. She slightly nods.* DECLAN *is oblivious.*

>   *As he continues to talk,* RENATA *slowly exits,* BOBBI *watching her every move as she does.*

Feelin' good about leavin' though. Don't have much time on this planet do yer, no. Anything could happen really, at any point. Anything could kill yer. Good to know when it's time to get it all done, live a proper life and that. Responsibility. Grab what you want from it all.

ACT TWO

    DECLAN *turns around.*

Yer know?
BOBBI: No time like the present.

    Beat.

How did you wind up with my keys that night?

    FLICK *and* JOHN *re-enter carrying an assortment of drinks.*

    BOBBI*'s eyes are on* DECLAN.

DECLAN: Could actually do with a drink I'm thinkin'. Might as well—
FLICK: She comin'?

    FLICK *hands* DECLAN *a drink.*

DECLAN: Yer, yer just cleanin' the baby up.
FLICK: Is Lily alright?
DECLAN: Yer, excited to go home / probably.
JOHN: Should we put on some like cool fresh beats / or something,
FLICK: Cool fresh beats?
JOHN: Yeah like some / Moby.

    DECLAN *pours himself a large drink and downs it in one.*

    The others pour drinks.

    A baby is heard crying.

DECLAN: Ooft. Wow. Yeah. Fuck / yeah.
JOHN: Yeah I was just saying maybe some Moby or / something.

    A baby crying.

DECLAN: Moby? Fuck outta here with that. [*Yelling*] Bring her out / Ren!

    FLICK *pulls out her phone, looking for music.*

    The baby continues crying.

FLICK: Metal! Let's put some metal on.
JOHN: Bit too peaceful here for metal, isn't it?
FLICK: It's the only thing that drowns out the noise!
JOHN: What noise?
DECLAN: [*yelling*] Ren! C'mon.
FLICK: Here we go!
JOHN: To Flick!

JOHN *raises his glass.*

FLICK *presses play and metal music plays.*

They each skull their drinks.

DECLAN *pours himself a second drink.*

He's hyped.

DECLAN: Fucken ... *fuck* yeah.

He begins to headbang / dance awkwardly.

The others watch him, perhaps joining in.

The following dialogue takes place over the volume of the music, the characters having to shout at each other.

It's been a real time, friends. What a fucken time. What a weird fucken place this is ah? I feel good. This is real music ah? Mmmph, man, some fucken diesel in my ears, fucken, mm-pha, mm-pha, chunky riffs and / shit, huh?

FLICK: Fucken diesel!

DECLAN: Throbbing through you, blasting. I'm out of control! Hah! You feel it, don't yer David!

JOHN: It's good! Kinda loud. But good actually. Actually, I love it!

A baby crying.

DECLAN: What is she—Ren! What's she doing?

FLICK: God I need to sit down a sec.

JOHN: I think that baby's crying.

DECLAN: I know she's crying. I'm not deaf, David. I know my baby.

DECLAN *exits.*

FLICK *lays down on one of the deckchairs.*

JOHN: [*to* FLICK] You alright?

FLICK: Yeah fine. Just weird ... gate's opening tomorrow. Everyone's probably leaving huh?

JOHN: I can't hear you—music's a bit loud. How do I—

FLICK: It's all good, I'm just feeling a bit ...

BOBBI: You think it's gonna storm, Flick?

DECLAN *re-enters holding the baby cot. He's furious.*

DECLAN: Where's she gone?

> DECLAN *scans the area.*

Fuckin' gone. Gone and left Lily alone again. Has she? Where is she?

JOHN: What is it?

FLICK: It's loud …

DECLAN: Answer me. Where's Ren?

FLICK: Maybe she's gone for a lie down.

> BOBBI *is watching* DECLAN.

JOHN: Maybe she went for a … wander.

> DECLAN *bends down to the cot, he's drunk.*

DECLAN: Where'd yer mama go hey? Gone for a wander has she? A wander-walk ah?

BOBBI: Maybe she's gone.

> JOHN *and* DECLAN *look at* BOBBI.
>
> *A small beat.*

JOHN: Maybe we should turn the music down.

DECLAN: [*to* BOBBI] What'd you say?

BOBBI: I said, maybe, she's gone. For good.

DECLAN: She'll be back. She's coming back. I know 'er.

BOBBI: Do you? Because I just watched her walk on out of here. Bag and everything this time.

> DECLAN *smacks Flick's phone.*
>
> *The music stops.*
>
> *No-one has realised that* FLICK *has fallen asleep.*

JOHN: [*quietly*] She did tell me she was planning on leaving today—

DECLAN: Fuck you know about it?

JOHN: She just told … me. Asked me to go with her—I should have said something … I mean I told her not to … She thinks there are devils here but they're not here—

DECLAN: Speak up, you quivering heap of junk. Look at yer.

JOHN: I just, I didn't think she would actually go … I mean she's a liar, isn't she? Can everyone admit she's a liar? Like she conned me.

Into coming here? And now she's running away. I don't even know what I'm doing here—
DECLAN: Pathetic shit you are. Talkin' garbage. What is *wrong* with all of you?
JOHN: I mean, you can't even smell blood.
DECLAN: Stop *saying* that! God it's hot, why is it so *fucking* hot in this place!
BOBBI: Best you calm down, Irish.
DECLAN: [*to* BOBBI] Did you speak to 'er?
BOBBI: Nope. Just watched her go.
DECLAN: That's great. That's brilliant. Let a young mother go and find herself in the wilderness with flesh eating dinosaurs. What about her baby ah?
BOBBI: She might be lookin' for somethin' better out there.
DECLAN: You don't know anything. Okay? You don't *really* know about the world do you?

Sittin' around in the same fucken place yer whole life, doin' nothin', learnin' nothin'.

You got no sense. You got no life.
BOBBI: She left. Not much I could do.
DECLAN: You're either stupid or heartless or both. You're a fucken numpty. How could you just do nothing?
BOBBI: [*yelling*] Good. Fucking. Question. Isn't it? You let my Mac die. You let my fucken Mac die like he was a piece of meat. You're weak. You're a little worm. You. Did. NOTHING.

> DECLAN *freezes, sorrow and shock choking him.*
>
> *As he opens his mouth,* FLICK *rises.*
>
> *She suddenly grabs the baby cot, submerging it in the pool.*
>
> BOBBI *and* JOHN *freeze in horror.*
>
> DECLAN *snaps out of his stupor among a cacophony of yelling.*
>
> *He pries the cot out of* FLICK*'s grasp, pulling it out of the water.*
>
> *He desperately rips it open and gently picks his daughter up, holding her against his chest.*
>
> *After several long beats, Lily cries.*
>
> *Blackout.*

EPILOGUE

Christmas Eve, morning. The pool area of The Palms Motel is eerily quiet. Eventually, DECLAN *enters, suitcase packed, baby strapped to his chest. He walks to the front of the stage, looks back at the motel, and exits.*

Lights down.

Lights up. Later in the day, JOHN *enters the pool area, bags packed. He exits to the motel gate. A moment later, he re-enters, waiting.*

FLICK *enters with* BOBBI. *A sad but joy-filled goodbye,* FLICK *and* BOBBI *hug.*

FLICK *passes* BOBBI *her promise voucher and whispers to her.*

BOBBI *nods.*

BOBBI *waves as* JOHN *and* FLICK *exit, together.*

Lights down.

Lights up.

A passing of time ensues. We watch an empty stage as it traverses through Christmas, New Year's Eve, the blistering heat of the summer, thunderstorms and torrential rain, until final calm ...

Then, weeks later.

RENATA *races on to the stage, a wild, triumphant smile on her face.*

RENATA: Flick? Flick?!

> *She looks around, slowly realising the emptiness. She begins to cry. A mixture of sadness and joy.*
>
> BOBBI *enters from the doorway. She beckons* RENATA *to join her inside before exiting.*
>
> *The stage dims, leaving* RENATA *sitting alone by the pool under the soft glow of the moon.*

THE END

www.ingramcontent.com/pod-product-compliance
Lightning Source LLC
Chambersburg PA
CBHW050019090426
42734CB00021B/3340